SENSATION AND PERCEPTION

EDITED BY

Richard L. Gregory
and
Andrew M. Colman

LONGMAN
London and New York

Longman Group Limited
Longman House, Burnt Mill
Harlow, Essex CM20 2JE, England
and Associated Companies throughout the world.

*Published in the United States of America
by Longman Publishing, New York*

© 1994 Routledge
This edition © 1995 Longman Group Limited
Compilation © 1995 Andrew Colman

This edition first published 1995

ISBN 0 582 27811 2 PPR

British Library Cataloguing-in-Publication Data
A catalogue record for this book is available from the British Library.

Library of Congress Cataloging-in-Publication Data
A catalogue record for this book is available from the Library of Congress.

Typeset by 25 in 10/12pt Times
Printed and bound by Bookcraft (Bath) Ltd

CONTENTS

v

NOTES ON EDITORS AND CONTRIBUTORS

ANDREW M. COLMAN is Reader in Psychology at the University of Leicester, having previously taught at Rhodes and Cape Town Universities in South Africa. He is the founder and former editor of the journal *Current Psychology* and Chief Examiner for the British Psychological Society's Qualifying Examination. His books include *Facts, Fallacies and Frauds in Psychology* (1987), *What is Psychology? The Inside Story* (2nd edn, 1988), and *Game Theory and its Applications in the Social and Biological Sciences* (2nd edn, 1995).

PETER C. DODWELL is Professor of Psychology at Queen's University, Kingston, Ontario. He was educated at Oxford University, receiving his doctorate in 1958. He has spent most of his professional career at Queen's, but has also taught at the University of London and at Harvard; he has held fellowships and other positions at universities in the United States, the United Kingdom, Australia, and New Zealand. He has been president of the Canadian Psychological Association, and edited the *Canadian Journal of Psychology* and *Spatial Vision*. He is a fellow of the Royal Society of Canada. He has published five books, including *Visual Pattern Recognition* (1970) and (as co-editor with T. M. Caelli) *Figural Synthesis* (1984).

RICHARD L. GREGORY is Emeritus Professor of Neuropsychology at the University of Bristol. He studied Moral Sciences at Cambridge, staying on to become a University Lecturer in the Department of Psychology and Fellow of Corpus Christi College. In 1967 he moved to Edinburgh to set up the Department of Machine Intelligence with Donald Mitchie and Christopher Longuet-Higgins. He moved to Bristol in 1970 to take up a Personal Chair in Neuropsychology and to become Director of the Brain and Perception Laboratory in the Medical School. He is the founder of the Exploratory Science Centre focused on astronomy at Herstmonceux Castle in East Sussex. He is a CBE and a Fellow of the Royal Society. His books include *The Intelligent Eye* (1970), *Mind in Science* (1981), *The Oxford Companion to the Mind*

(1987), and *Eye and Brain* (4th edn, 1990). He is the founder and editor of the journal *Perception*.

MIKE G. HARRIS obtained his PhD in psychology from the University of Bristol in 1980, after undergraduate courses in medical physiology and neurobiology, and several years as a professional musician. Since 1980 he has taught perception at the University of Birmingham, where he is currently Head of the Cognitive Science MSc course and a Director of the Cognitive Science Research Centre. His research interests centre on the psychophysical and computational study of early visual processes, with a particular interest in the analysis and usage of retinal motion, and cricket.

GLYN W. HUMPHREYS obtained a BSc and PhD from the University of Bristol. From 1979 to 1989 he was a Lecturer, then Senior Lecturer and Professor, in the Department of Psychology at Birkbeck College, London. Since 1989 he has been Professor of Cognitive Psychology at the University of Birmingham, where he is currently Head of the School of Psychology. He was the editor of the *Quarterly Journal of Experimental Psychology* from 1989 to 1993, and is a board member of *Cognitive Neuropsychology, Mind and Language*, and the *Journal of Experimental Psychology: Human Perception and Performance*. He initiated a new journal of *Visual Cognition*, beginning in 1994. His research interests are in the interlocking of cognitive science, cognitive neuropsychology and experimental psychology, particularly in the field of visual cognition.

DONALD LAMING is Lecturer in Experimental Psychology at the University of Cambridge. He is the author of *Information Theory of Choice-Reaction Times* (1968), *Mathematical Psychology* (1973), and *Sensory Analysis* (1986). He is currently engaged on a book which applies the principles of sensory judgement to social issues.

BRIAN C. J. MOORE is Reader in Auditory Perception in the Department of Experimental Psychology, University of Cambridge. He is a fellow of the Acoustical Society of America and a Visiting Consulting Professor in the Department of Bioengineering, University of Ulster. He is the author of *An Introduction to the Psychology of Hearing* (3rd edn, 1989).

HARVEY RICHARD SCHIFFMAN is Professor of Psychology at Rutgers, The State University, New Brunswick, New Jersey. He received his PhD from the University of North Carolina at Chapel Hill. He has published articles on space perception, visual illusions, and the perception of time. He is the author of *Sensation and Perception: An Integrated Approach* (3rd edn, 1990).

SERIES EDITOR'S PREFACE

The *Longman Essential Psychology* series comprises twelve concise and inexpensive paperback volumes covering all of the major topics studied in undergraduate psychology degree courses. The series is intended chiefly for students of psychology and other subjects with psychology components, including medicine, nursing, sociology, social work, and education. Each volume contains five or six accessibly written chapters by acknowledged authorities in their fields, and each chapter includes a list of references and a small number of recommendations for further reading.

Most of the material was prepared originally for the Routledge *Companion Encyclopedia of Psychology* but with a view to later paperback subdivision – the contributors were asked to keep future textbook readers at the front of their minds. Additional material has been added for the paperback series: new co-editors have been recruited for nine of the volumes that deal with highly specialized topics, and each volume has a new introduction, a glossary of technical terms including a number of entries written specially for this edition, and a comprehensive new index.

I am grateful to my literary agents Sheila Watson and Amanda Little for clearing a path through difficult terrain towards the publication of this series, to Sarah Caro of Longman for her patient and efficient preparation of the series, to Brian Parkinson, David Stretch, and Susan Dye for useful advice and comments, and to Carolyn Preston for helping with the compilation of the glossaries.

ANDREW M. COLMAN

INTRODUCTION

Richard L. Gregory
University of Bristol, England

Andrew M. Colman
University of Leicester, England

When we open our eyes, colours and objects appear immediately without apparent effort, so one might think that nothing much is going on in the brain — that perception is simply mirroring the external world. The ancient Greeks were the first to give serious consideration to perception two and a half thousand years ago, and it was they who first realized that the eyes cannot see and the ears cannot hear without internal representations, which are now known to be located in the brain (see Gregory, 1981, ch. 12). Since then it has become more and more clear that processes of seeing and hearing and so on are not at all simple, and also that they are not altogether reliable. There is, indeed, an intelligence to perception: it involves complex problem solving and does not always get the right answer. The eyes have imperfect images; the skin has depressions from objects in contact; the ears receive vibrations of the air; the nose analyses particles chemically. But what we experience is far more than pictures and touches and vibrations and dust. What we experience is an incredibly rich world of interacting objects, most of which are largely hidden and all inadequately represented to the senses. From the optical images in our eyes we can handle and interact with objects according to their non-visual characteristics — weight, hardness, edibility, breakability and so on. In a theatre we see bits of heads and faces of the audience, because the people further away are largely hidden by the nearer. We assume that people are complete and have backs to their heads. From the back of a head, we assume a hidden face. It is a frightening experience for

xi

someone to wear a mask at the back of the head and rotate slowly to face us, creating a face where no face should be.

The present emphasis on creative activity of perception, and its need for topping up sensory data by assumptions from knowledge stored from the past, is a radical change from the British empiricist tradition in philosophy. The empiricists, such as Hume, Berkeley and Locke, thought that perception was directly related to the world of objects, and that it was therefore reliable as the source of all knowledge. Philosophers have almost always based theories of knowledge on assumed perceptual certainty. We now know, however, that there is an extremely rich world of illusion.

A case in point is the size-weight illusion (see for example, Jones, 1986, 1988). Experiments have shown that when two objects are of equal weight but one is much smaller than the other, almost everyone who lifts them judges the smaller object to be much heavier than the larger one and feels certain that this is the case. In one experiment in the United States, 100 military officers judged (on average) the smaller object to be more than twice the weight of the larger one, which was twice as wide and deep but the same weight. This shows that a pound of feathers certainly *feels* much lighter than a pound of lead and that people who rely on subjective judgements of weight when they go shopping are liable to make serious mistakes.

In visual perception, it is very easy to create false ghosts and all manner of distortions of size and distance. By looking at "ambiguous" pictures and objects, we learn that there are rival hypotheses waiting to take over centre stage. Indeed, one may think of perceptions themselves as hypotheses of objects – much like hypotheses in science, suggested and tested by data and enriched by knowledge and assumption. This, at least, is one current way of interpreting perception (Gregory, 1980, 1990).

It was generally believed that perceptions are made up of sensations. Following the physiological discovery, early this century, that neural information is transmitted by neural "action potentials" (tiny pulses of electricity running along nerves, the frequency of firing increasing with intensity), we now think of the raw data of perception not as sensation, but rather as physiological – information coded by activity in nerves. It is a short step to think of the mind not as separate from the brain, but rather as the result of electrical and chemical brain activity. With our present familiarity with computers, it is also a small step to think of the mind as somewhat like software of (physiological) computers of the nervous system. This means that to understand we need to appreciate both the physiology (squishyware) and the cognitive rules and stored data handled by the brain.

It remains exceedingly mysterious why we have sensations – that is, awareness – of what are now called by philosophers *qualia* of red, pain, and the piquancy of pilchards. We have come a long way from the ancient idea, that sensation is primary, to the current view that it is physical events in the nervous system that signal and store information and carry out somewhat computer-like processes, except that the sensations that seemed so obvious and not worth questioning are now the biggest mystery!

This volume deals with material from the oldest field of psychological research, and it is not altogether easy or simple – it cannot be. But it contains a lot of information and suggests even more questions. In chapter 1, Peter C. Dodwell outlines processes of how we see. This raises an issue that recurs continually in psychology: how much of perception and behaviour is given from innate inherited knowledge? How far is it due to what each of us has to learn from infancy onwards? Over the last thirty or so years this pendulum has swung from the assumption that almost all is inherited to the view that a great deal has to be learned. It remains difficult to establish just what is inherited and what learned; but it is remarkable that extremely young babies can copy their mothers' facial expressions, which suggests that the infant world is more than the "blooming, buzzing confusion" envisaged by Williams James a century ago.

In chapter 2, Mike G. Harris and Glyn W. Humphreys describe the extremely influential work of the late David Marr. This is central to discussions of artificial intelligence (AI) and how machines might be made to see and behave appropriately towards objects. David Marr stressed the processing of information "upwards", but as Harris and Humphreys say, another pendulum has swung in favour of very considerable "bottom-down" cognitive contributions for making sense of natural and artificial senses. The current state of technology can have deep effects on philosophical and scientific accounts. Now that computers can handle and store vast amounts of information, with increasing rapidity for making associations – though they are still incapable of making puns! – we may expect to see a further swing of this pendulum, towards massive top-down contributions for perception. For readers who wish to go further into this topic, a book by Mitchie (1994) on computational analysis of visual motion may be of interest.

In chapter 3, Brian C. J. Moore offers a rich survey of hearing: the structure and function of the incredible mechanisms of the ear, its ability to signal loudness and pitch and the rich range of timbre of musical instruments and voices. The sensitivity of the ear is almost beyond belief: experiments have shown that hair cells in the inner ear begin to trigger nerve impulses when their tips move one ten-thousandth of a millimetre. Hearing has not been studied as thoroughly as vision, partly because it is technically more difficult and its relevant regions of the brain are less available for electrophysiological recording. Deafness is a very common and severe problem, capable of ruining careers and causing personality problems as communication gets more difficult. In Britain alone there are over a million people suffering from handicapping hearing impairment. So far, hearing aids are nothing like as effective as spectacles are for correcting optical errors of the eyes. Part of the problem (which was exactly the same in the early decades of glasses) is vanity. People seek invisible hearing aids rather than accept something larger that actually works. Indeed, wearing a string dangling from the ear is extremely effective – it makes one's friends speak louder and more clearly! For a more detailed account of the psychology of hearing, see Moore (1995) or, for a different approach, McAdams and Bigand (1993).

In chapter 4, Harvey Richard Schiffman discusses the skin senses: touch and pressure, temperature and pain, and one might include tickle. As for the all the senses, touch turns out to be far more complicated than expected. Some sensations are "primary"; while others, such as "stickiness", are compounded from simpler signals. There is a long history of seeking physiologically simple colours, tastes, smells, and touches, and discovering laws of mixtures. What seem to be simple sensations can often turn out to be physiologically complex.

Finally, in chapter 5, Donald Laming explains the methods and findings of psychophysics. Psychophysics attempts to use some of the methods of measurement and statistical analysis of physics to discover how external stimuli are related to internal sensation. This borders on metaphysics; but perhaps this is true also of astronomers' questions about the beginning of time and the basis of physical laws. Generally, as more powerful techniques become available, the frontiers of metaphysics are pushed back. Donald Laming's work lies at the edge of our understanding of the relations between mind and matter. This involves mathematics. And just why mathematics works so well has its own mysteries; is mathematics a creation of mind or is it inherent in the structure of the universe? For a more extended account of psychophysics, especially in relation to auditory perception, see Yost, Popper, and Fay (1993).

We should not forget context and the effect of what we happen to be doing when we perceive things. It is striking how appalling coffee tastes when one assumes it to be tea, or tea believed to be coffee. There is far more to seeing than meets the eye, and far more to hearing, touch, and taste, than meets the other receptors of the nervous system. Creativity starts with the intelligence of perception.

In addition to the publications mentioned in this introduction, the suggestions for further reading at the end of each chapter will be helpful for readers who wish to delve more deeply into the various aspects of sensation and perceptions covered in this slim volume.

REFERENCES

Gregory, R. L. (1980). Perceptions as hypotheses. *Philosophical Transactions of the Royal Society of London, Series B – Biological Sciences, 290*, 191–7.

Gregory, R. L. (1981). *Mind in science: A history of explanations in psychology and physics*. London: Weidenfeld and Nicholson.

Gregory, R. L. (1990). *Eye and brain: The psychology of seeing* (4th edn.). Oxford: Oxford University Press.

INTRODUCTION

Jones L. A. (1986). Perception of force and weight: Theory and research. *Psychological Bulletin*, *100*, 29–42.

Jones, L. A. (1988). Motor illusions: What do they reveal about proprioception?. *Psychological Bulletin*, *103*, 72–86.

McAclams, S., & Bigand, E. (eds). (1993). *Thinking in sound: The cognitive psychology of human audition*. Oxford: Oxford University Press.

Mitchie, A. (1994). *Computational analysis of visual motion*. New York: Plenum.

Moore, B. C. J. (1995). *Hearing*. San Diego, CA: Academic Press.

Yost, W. A., Popper, A. N., & Fay, R. R. (1993). (eds). *Human psychophysics*. New York: Springer-Verlag.

1

FUNDAMENTAL PROCESSES IN VISION

Peter C. Dodwell

Queen's University, Ontario, Canada

Reading a book, hearing a familiar song, recognizing a friend's face – all are characteristic acts of perception which occur so effortlessly that we take them for granted. Yet the study of perception is a major field in modern psychology, and one that is full of new and interesting challenges. In order to understand the processes of seeing we have to understand the nature of the physical events that give rise to perception, the physiological processes that record them, and the psychological abilities of the perceiver that make sense of them.

Perception is the primary process by means of which we obtain knowledge of the world: it has been estimated that more than 80 per cent of it is accounted for by vision. Certainly the visual system is by far the most thoroughly studied of the senses (conventionally five are recognized: sight, hearing, taste, touch, and smell) and the best understood. Perception is a skill, or set of skills, not simply the passive recording of external stimulation

(Gibson, 1966). A perceiving organism is more like a map-reader than a camera. What we so easily accept in perceiving and understanding the world involves complex processes at many levels. Psychological research on seeing extends all the way from the study of the electrical activity of single cells in the eye or brain, to colour vision, the perception of objects and events, learning to read, and understanding the complexity of an air traffic controller's video console.

The early investigation of perception, as with so much of psychology, started with philosophical speculation about how the senses work, and what role they might play in the acquisition of knowledge. Much of this early work involved intellectual justification for claiming that our senses supply reliable and valid knowledge about the world and ourselves. It was only in the middle of the nineteenth century that the scientific and experimental study of these matters came into being, and some of the first psychological laboratories were established in Germany for the study of the senses, including vision, in the second half of the nineteenth century (Boring, 1950).

NATIVISM AND EMPIRICISM

Two themes dominated the early psychological research on vision, themes that were derived from established philosophical traditions. On the one hand there was the view, derived from the British *empiricist* philosophers of the seventeenth and eighteenth centuries, principally John Locke (1632–1704), George Berkeley (1685–1753), and David Hume (1711–1776), that all our knowledge is based ultimately on the senses, the elementary sensations being as it were the building blocks of knowledge, all else being secondary, influenced by habit, assumption, memory, and the like. These would help to build up our representation of the world – this view is also called "constructivist" – but the primary elements of knowledge are even so given in the simple "raw" sensations.

In contrast was the nativist position, deriving from the rationalism of the French philosopher René Descartes (1596–1650), which claimed that the senses are fallible, all true knowledge thus needing to be grounded in clear thinking, reasoning, and the innate capacity to order and refine the messages of the senses. These opposed views are still reflected in the theoretical and practical activities of modern psychologists, but in the 1890s they dominated the field to a remarkable degree. On the one hand Hermann von Helmholtz (1821–1894), the great physicist and psychologist, held that all sensory stimulation is inherently ambiguous, and true perception required the active participation of the perceiver in order to succeed (he called this process "unconscious inference"), and on the other hand stood the physiologist Ewald Hering (1834–1918), champion of the notion that understanding of psychological processes was mainly dependent on the investigation of the neural activity supporting it, thus having an innate basis.

2

In the present day, it would be difficult to find a supporter of either of these positions in their simple form, but they still exist as the poles, as it were, of the spectrum of theoretical positions perceptual psychologists adopt. It is now much more a matter of investigating the manner in which innate processes interact with, or are influenced by, experience of different kinds, and in this regard we shall see that much progress has been made.

THE PHYSIOLOGY OF THE VISUAL SYSTEM

There is a well-defined area of the brain and its associated "inputs" which is known as the primary visual system (Dreher & Robinson, 1991). It is illustrated in Figure 1. The eyes are, of course, the organs by means of which we gain visual access to the world; we say that light is the "adequate stimulus" to vision. Visual sensations can be produced in other ways, for example by

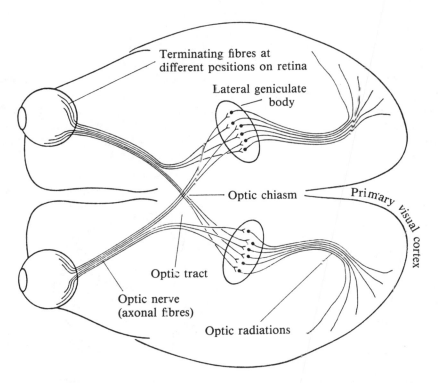

Figure 1   The basic layout of the human "primary visual system", greatly simplified. Light enters the eyes, is captured and transduced into physiological signals at the retina, which is a multi-layered neural complex at the back of the eye. These signals are transmitted to the visual area of the brain, also called the occipital cortex

3

chemical, thermal, or mechanical means, but these do not supply reliable and interpretable information about the world in the same way as light. A great deal is known about the physiological substrate to vision and this knowledge is fundamental to our understanding of how we see, what constitutes "normal" perception, and how the mature perceptual system develops.

The central nervous system is made up of many sorts of specialized cells, or neurons, which record, transmit, and modify signals that are essentially electrical pulses. Neurons are connected together, and the manner and place of these connections determine different physiological systems. In the case of vision, specialized neurons in the retina of the eye receive light, and cause neural signals to be generated that are transmitted through the various pathways (illustrated in Figure 1) to the posterior portion of the brain. Notice that there are various relay stations on the way to the brain cortex, at which information is sorted and refined. Of particular importance are the retina, that light-sensitive area at the back of the eye on to which light is focused by the optical lens at the front of the eye (see Figure 2) and the lateral geniculate bodies of the midbrain, where signals from the two eyes are first "mixed". The whole anatomical and physiological basis for vision is one of extraordinary complexity and delicacy, and it is mainly since the early 1960s that a detailed knowledge of how it works has been attained.

The major breakthrough came with the ability to record from single neurons in different parts of the system, starting with its peripheral part, namely the retina of the eye, and culminating in the impressive work of David Hubel and Torsten Wiesel of Harvard University who, in 1962, first reported on recordings from single neurons in the brain cortex of the cat. For this they justly earned a Nobel Prize (Hubel & Wiesel, 1962).

The interconnections of neurons in the brain are so dense and complex that

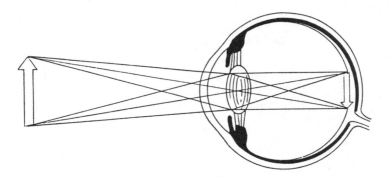

Figure 2 A diagram of the eyeball. Light enters through the pupil and is focused into sharp images on the retina by the lens. This part of the visual apparatus is much like a camera; or perhaps we should more truthfully say that the camera is like an eye

one might well despair of ever being able to understand what the function of individual neurons might be. Yet the remarkable discovery of Hubel and Wiesel was that usually this function is not too difficult to describe and analyse. Before them it had been widely accepted that the connections at birth between neurons must be essentially random, and that it would be the function of experience to "tune up" the system so that it could deal adequately with the information supplied to it through the eyes. Indeed this was the basis of a celebrated and widely accepted theory of perceptual learning due to the Canadian psychologist D. O. Hebb (1949). These developments are discussed in Dodwell (1970).

Hubel and Wiesel were able to show that most neurons in the primary visual area of the brain are specialized so that they respond to quite specific features of the environment. Like the ganglion cells of the retina, each cortical cell has a *retinal receptive field*, that is, a circumscribed and usually small area of the retina to which it responds. Moreover most of them are activated by short lines at a particular orientation within the receptive field. For example, there are some cells that respond to a horizontal line at the centre of the visual field, others prefer vertical or diagonal lines in other parts of the field, and so on. The important point is that they all have a definite preference, which can be quite readily defined. What the role of these *feature detectors* may be in the larger scheme of visual perception, and how they are to be understood as the building blocks for the development of a mature perceiving organism, are questions we shall defer for the moment. One of the most telling of Hubel and Wiesel's discoveries was the fact that the high degree of specificity in *stimulus coding*, as it is called, is innate in the kitten. They found that young kittens, prior to any visual experience, have in place a coding system with many of the features of adult vision. To be sure it is not so precise, and it can be modified to some degree by experience, but basically the system is in place at birth. There is good reason to suppose that what is true of the kitten is true of other mammals, including humans. Thus the empiricism of the psychologist Hebb was to a great extent overtaken by the discoveries of Hubel and Wiesel (and subsequently very many other investigators) concerning the actual physiological mechanisms in place at birth.

Does this mean that nativism has won the day? No, because we shall see later that the built-in coding system is itself subject to modification in the light of experience. This will demonstrate how in modern research the simplistic division between nativism and empiricism has been replaced by a far more sophisticated and informative account of how innate factors interact with experienced events to shape the mature visual system − and the adult perceiver (Cronly-Dillon, 1991).

Since Hubel and Wiesel's discoveries, much more has been discovered about how the visual brain works. The different sensory qualities of contour, movement, colour, and depth have all been found to be processed in anatomically distinct "channels" which even have separate "maps" in different

5

parts of the brain cortex (Maunsell & Newsome, 1987). Certain "higher order" neurons that are sensitive to more complicated aspects of the visual field than simple oriented line segments have been identified, even some that respond to hands, moving human bodies, and faces (Perrett et al., 1985)! We shall have to pass over this exciting work in the interest of describing other important and less specialized aspects of the visual system.

This brief survey of the physiological basis of vision has shown that the broad outline of the areas of the brain involved in seeing are well known, and that the detailed operation of many of the individual parts is understood, at least as far as the operations of the neurons in them is concerned. This is only a basis, however, and there is much more to learn about the nature of seeing, and how its properties have been investigated and understood.

THE VISUAL WORLD: SPACE AND OBJECT PERCEPTION

The most obvious property of our visual world is that it is extended in space and time. The spatial character is to be understood in terms of the formation of a sharp image of the visual scene on the retina of the eye (Figure 2). This spatial image is reproduced, at least approximately, in the visual cortex of the brain (Figure 1). We call the image in the eye the "retinal image"; some but by no means all the properties of seeing can be understood in terms of it. The retinal image depends on the optical properties of both the environment and the eye. As Figure 3 shows, the size of the image depends on the distance between eye and object, but we know very well that perceived size does not vary to anything like the degree to be expected in these terms. Your friends do not suddenly shrink in size as they move away from you! This discrepancy between what the retinal image might lead one to expect, and the actual "phenomenological" appearance (that is, how things really appear to the observer) is called *perceptual constancy*, and occurs not only for size, but also for shape, colour, and brightness, among others. In each case what is meant by constancy is the fact that what one sees (the phenomenon) is far *less* variable than what an analysis of the optical and other physical features of the stimulating environment would lead one to expect. To take another

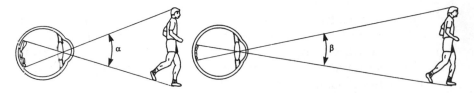

Figure 3 The retinal image, and visual angle. The size of the retinal image is measured in terms of *visual angle*, which is clearly dependent on both physical size, and distance

example, consider the appearance of a book with a blue cover. You look at it in bright daylight, or in the artificial illumination of a neon lamp, you stretch out the arm that holds it, or turn it away from you. In each case the stimulation reaching your retina implies (if it does not demand) that what you see should vary markedly. Yet what you do see is a book with quite stable visual characteristics. Constancy has done its job without your cooperation or awareness. It is factors of this sort that led Helmholtz to talk of "unconscious inference", and empiricists generally to question whether a simple account of the physiological processing systems involved could ever reach a satisfactory account of the nature of perception (Rock, 1984).

A more general aspect of the empiricist stance, stemming from the views of Bishop Berkeley, one of the empiricist philosophers who did so much to establish one pole of the theoretical debate discussed above, is this: the retinal image is essentially *ambiguous*; many different stimulus configurations could in principle give rise to one and the same retinal image (a wine bottle viewed from 50 cm versus a half-bottle viewed from 40 cm, for example). Therefore some *non-visual* information must be added to the visual to achieve veridical perception. The roles of different cues, both visual and non-visual, in achieving both a true representation of the world, and in manipulating our perceptions in amusing and sometimes confusing ways, were explored by a group of American psychologists who called themselves *transactionalists*. For them perception was a transaction between observer and environment — yet another twist on the empiricist theme (Kilpatrick, 1961). Results of their research can be seen in the distorted rooms and similar illusory displays to be found in many a science centre. The best known of these is a distorted room in which, from a certain vantage point, the retinal image is identical to that which would be produced by a normal "four square" room. When the room is viewed from this point, it does indeed appear normal, and we may have difficulty in being persuaded otherwise. In such a room strong illusions of size and distance can be induced. All this shows with remarkable force how easy it is to manipulate visual cues to yield non-veridical percepts. It demonstrates how much we are creatures of habit, in this case the cognitive habits induced by the properties of our stable visual surroundings.

Our perceptual world is indeed usually very stable, yields few surprises, and is not subject to misinterpretation. No doubt this is why non-psychologists normally pay little attention to how they perceive, and may be surprised that there is so much about perception that requires investigation and explanation. It is stable because most of our percepts are *overdetermined*; visual cues are mutually consistent and are reinforced by tactile, auditory, and other information about what is in the world. Only a philosopher would question whether the object in front of us is really a solid table, or the person we're talking to a robot. The world is just too consistent for us to worry about such things. But it is still true that we take a great deal on trust. It is not difficult to break the trust, and doing so can be revealing.

PERCEPTUAL ILLUSIONS

Everyone is familiar with visual illusions of different types. A small sample of the best known is shown in Figures 4–6. Far from being mere party amusements, these illusions can help us to understand quite a bit about perception. First, why do we call them illusions? Because, as with the distorted room, there is a discrepancy between what common sense, habit, or geometrical intuition tells us should be seen, and what we actually see. Consider the Müller-Lyer illusion of Figure 4a. The two horizontal lines are of equal length, yet are seen as different. It has been proposed that the illusion is induced by false intimations of perspective (as in the Ponzo illusion, Figure 4e), yet this cannot be the whole story, as other versions of the Müller-Lyer, as in Figure 4b–d, do not share the perspective interpretation. Perhaps illusions are caused by the way information is coded by physiological mechanisms in some cases, or by the way the layout is interpreted, or by simple misinterpretation of distance cues. Study of the illusions is important, but the fact is they seem to raise almost as many questions as they answer. No one theory of the illusions has gained universal acceptance; perhaps their main challenge is in reminding us of the many different factors that can enter into perceptual processing, and alerting us to the need to be flexible in thinking about how we come to know the world through seeing.

Some aspects of perception can be understood if we know about the coding

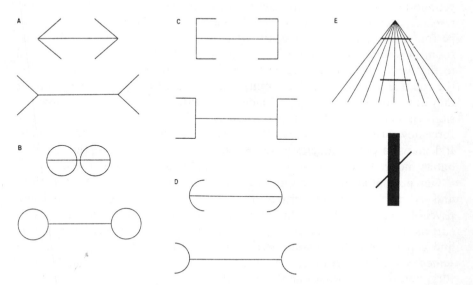

Figure 4 Some of the best-known simple visual illusions (of which there are hundreds). 4a, the Müller-Lyer illusion, is perhaps the best known, and most studied, of them all. 4b–d show some variations on the same theme. Figure 4e is the Ponzo illusion (top) and the Poggendorf (bottom)

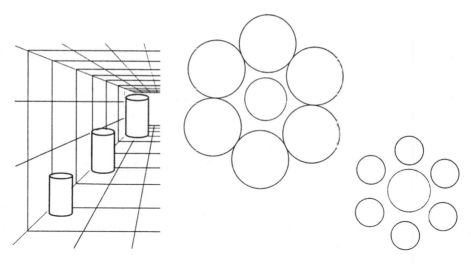

Figure 5 Two illusions of size, induced by context; the one case by perspective (giving a false impression of distance, so "size constancy" is operative), in the other distortion is due to strong relative size cues

of features, as in colour vision or the elementary contour elements as studied by Hubel and Wiesel. Others require an understanding of how different cues, to depth and distance for instance, interact to affect what is seen (Figure 5). Still others, like the distorted room, require us to consider how our habits of thought and expectations – unconscious inferences – determine what we see. The study of illusion is like a workshop for the meshing together of all the different sorts of influence that bear on perception.

GESTALT PSYCHOLOGY

The study of illusions certainly seems to favour an eclectic and empiricist approach to perception. Yet there have been influential movements in psychology that have denied that position. Gestalt psychology was one of them; it asserted the primacy of organizational phenomena, yet denied the role of experience in building up perception. The German word *Gestalt* means "configuration", and identifies the main tenet of that school of psychology, namely that the nature of perception is *holistic*; it is not to be understood by breaking it into elementary parts. The elements of Figure 6a and b for example fall "naturally" into a certain organization. We seem to have no control over this, and it occurs without effort on our part. The Gestalt psychologists maintained that this is no accident; for them the visual field was determined by a set of organizational principles that are simply a part of the way the brain works (Köhler, 1929). This school of psychology arose at a

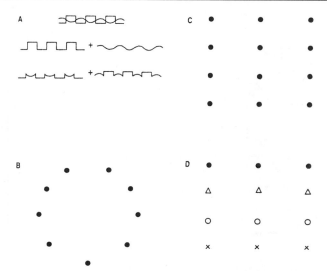

Figure 6 Four classical Gestalt demonstrations of "natural" perceptual organization. In 6a, the top form is organized into a "square wave" and a "sinusoid" rather
than into the equally possible decomposition shown at the bottom of the figure. No
one would fail to see the circular organization of 6b. In 6c organization into columns
is mediated by proximity, but in 6d the proximity is overridden by similarity of the
elements in each row. There are a dozen or so Gestalt "principles" of organization,
that seem to describe most instances of such natural organization

time when little was known about the operations of the visual brain. Indeed
Gestalt psychologists held theories about brain activity that are now known
to be false. For this reason the school fell into disrepute, yet it provided a
brilliant set of demonstrations of organizational phenomena in perception
that are still valid, and pose a challenge to modern theories of perception.
Figure 7 illustrates some displays with a strong Gestalt flavour (commonly
true of many cartoons, incidentally), but if one thinks about it, the organization here is not merely automatic, it relies on our interpretation of the elements in the displays. In fact a major weakness of the Gestalt theory was its
failure to take account of the many factors that impinge on perception.
Indeed it denied them, and was quite nativistic in approach. It is worth a
place in the history of perception, however, not only for the power of the
demonstrations it spawned, but also as a warning of the dangers of being too
narrow in the range of influences one is willing to allow in trying to understand perception. There was a resurgence of interest in the Gestalt approach
some years ago (see Kubovy & Pomerantz, 1981).

10

Figure 7 There are strong Gestalt principles at work in these cartoons, but notice that they also depend on a strong element of interpretation (meaningfulness) for their effect

GIBSON'S PERCEPTUAL THEORY

The theoretical position of J. J. Gibson was strongly influenced by Gestalt psychology, although in some ways it was very different (Gibson, 1950, 1966). He, like the Gestalt theorists, was disenchanted by the traditional empiricist approach in which elements of sensory experience are somehow glued together to yield the coherent, one-piece perceptual world of normal experience. What is this glue? Nobody knows. Gibson argued that it is unnecessary to know, because the glue does not exist. He came to this conclusion as a young US Air Force psychologist during the Second World War, attempting to use his knowledge of the psychology of perception to aid in the training of pilots. Traditional theory was of no help, but he was struck by the fact that the information they *used* in flying their machines was nevertheless readily identified and described. Given this background, it is not surprising that Gibson concentrated his attention on movement, and concluded that information contained in moving displays (in traditional terms, the motion of the retinal image) was of decisive importance, for instance in the landing of an aircraft. From this he reached the idea that information in "whole field" displays gives valid and salient information about the true state of the world.

Here is an example of a typical Gibsonian demonstration: take a wire coathanger and bend it into an arbitrary, but fairly complicated, shape. "Shadowcast" this on a screen with a single light source, and have an observer view the screen only. What will be seen is a flat squiggly shape. Now start to rotate the hanger (about a vertical axis), and the three-dimensional nature of the shape "leaps out". This has all the punch and convincingness of a Gestalt demonstration. No analysis of the local element movements gives the effect. It is a true "whole-field" phenomenon. Gibson argued that such whole field displays very often contained *gradients* of information, in the case of motion the different parts of the field would move at different rates, thereby signalling the true layout of the world. Figure 8 gives an indication of another such motion gradient. Other gradients, for example of perspective and texture, were likewise held to be the basis for veridical perception, as in Figure 9.

In his early work, Gibson called this "global psychophysics", the idea being that the visual stimulation arising from the world had a coherence that was not dependent on the observer's own knowledge or activity (one sees the close relationship to Gestalt theory) but was inherent in what he called the *optic array*, that is, the physical structure of the light impinging on the observer's eye (rather than being a function of brain organization, as in the Gestalt account). All this is very true, and there is no doubt that Gibson's ideas had a fundamental effect on our understanding of the nature of perception, and especially on the importance of analysing the stimulus properties to which organisms are sensitive, and to which they respond. This aspect of his work has had a profound influence in a surprising place, namely in the

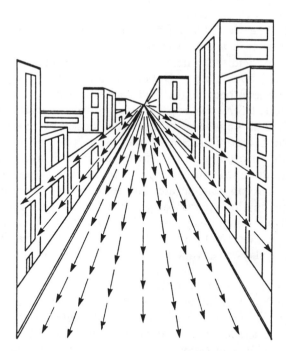

Figure 8 An indication of the movement gradients generated by "straight ahead" motion of the observer. The relative velocity of different elements in the field is indicated by the lengths of the arrows. Such relative motion provides gradients of stimulation that contain valid information about the world, as Gibson demonstrated

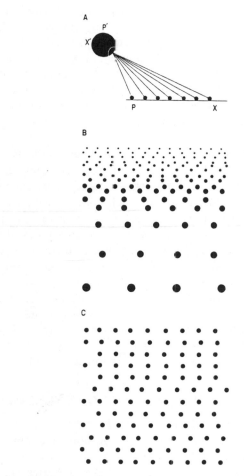

Figure 9 Texture gradients also give strong cues to depth and slant. 9a indicates how, optically, the texture of 9b would be generated. 9c has ro texture gradient, and supplies no depth information

field of computational and machine vision, and artificial intelligence (see Banks & Krajicek, 1991).

Gibson was successful in demonstrating the important role gradients can play in perception. As with any successful theory, however, there is a danger of claiming too much. While a great deal can be understood in these terms, it is going too far to claim, as Gibson did, that the whole of perception can be captured in this net. There are phenomena of constancy, and the illusions, which do not fit easily into the Gibsonian view. Likewise it would be difficult to account for more symbolic perceptual activities like reading, or artistic representation, along these lines.

13

Gibson always claimed that his ideas were powerful enough to encompass everything, but his programme was never wholly successful. On the other hand his influence has been great, and beneficial. By insisting on the careful definition of the properties of the light impinging on the eye he established a new standard of perceptual analysis. Like the Gestalt psychologists he insisted on the organized quality of our perceptions, but unlike them he was not at all interested in the physiological substrate of perception. He felt that undue concern with that substrate would tend to make us ask the wrong questions about perception.

Gibson was very modern in his insistence that perception is to be understood as the basis for action, for defining the ecological niche of the organism, and for understanding both organism and environment as a single interacting system. He argued that too much concern with the physiology would simply displace concern from the places where it was most needed. In view of the amazing advances in knowledge of the physiological substrate in recent years, and the extent to which it has influenced practical and theoretical understanding of vision, this stance may seem bizarre, yet we owe an immense debt of gratitude to Gibson for freeing us from the "piecemeal, instantaneous frozen section" view of sensory stimulation that was the traditional view before his time. It is now understood that the dynamic, whole-field sensory continuum contains far richer sources of information than we thought (Cutting, 1987; Wallach, 1987). Modern research has capitalized on this change in the way stimulation is treated.

PERCEPTUAL PLASTICITY AND LEARNING

Both Gestalt psychology and Gibson's theory deny the role of "constructive" learning in perception, yet there is a long tradition, and ample evidence, attesting to its importance. Following the lead provided by Hebb (1949), a vast amount of research has been done to assess the matter. This has been of several kinds, including work on perceptual development in infancy and with young animals raised in specialized environments, and studying the ways in which adults respond to distortions of their normal perceptual "diet". The findings complement other methods of studying perception in mature organisms.

Initial work, starting in the early 1960s, attempted to assess the effects of restriction on the rearing of young animals. Thus kittens, for example, were raised in the dark for some weeks or months, and an assessment was then made of their visual capacities. The results were inconclusive, because it was never possible to prove that the visual apparatus was functioning properly after such treatment. But surely the point of such research was to show that the system was not normal? The problem was that researchers were looking for changes that could be attributed to lack of experience, which were expected to occur in the brain, but the damage caused by restricted vision

14

probably was also occurring in the periphery (at the retina, for example). In that case even if central (brain) malfunction had been induced, there was no way of separating its effects from the peripheral effects, so the results were bound to be of little theoretical interest. A more promising approach was to rear animals in specialized environments rather than just in the dark, and to look for changes in behaviour subsequently. A number of ingenious studies along these lines were undertaken, especially in the laboratory of Richard Held at Brandeis University, and subsequently at the Massachusetts Institute of Technology (Held, 1965). The tests of visual function were behavioural and functional and had some intriguing results, but a still more promising line of attack became available with the development of the single-neuron recording methods described above.

Hubel and Wiesel had shown, even in their first classic paper, that many of the neurons in the cat's visual cortex are binocular, that is to say, a given neuron would have receptive fields in both eyes, so could be made to respond to similar features presented to either the left or the right eye not only separately, but also in combination. This implies an amazing degree of coordination in the anatomical arrangements, even in the newborn kitten. They found, by a technique of restricted rearing, that the balance between the two eyes could be disrupted. A kitten reared with artificial squint, so that the coordination between the eyes was lost, no longer showed regular binocular responding. This work was taken further by others who were able to show that kittens (and other mammals) could be reared so as to produce essentially two "monocular" visual brains, that is, to have no neurons capable of responding to both eyes, and indeed having a restricted capacity to respond only to a limited set of visual features, such as horizontal contours in one eye, vertical in the other. Of great interest is the fact that the plasticity of the brain is greatest in the very young organism (about the first three months of life in the kitten) and later on disappears almost entirely. This and similar work is reviewed in Blakemore (1978). This work led to the study of binocular abnormalities in human infants, and to programmes attempting to relieve such conditions.

Research on plasticity shows how new techniques have made it possible to answer old questions in new ways, and to cast light on matters of theoretical as well as practical significance. It also shows how psychological questions can become the province of other scientists' research, which in turn leads to further psychological advance.

A somewhat different approach to plasticity is found in studies of adult responses to novel stimulation. In the 1890s George Stratton asked what the perceptual effect of inverting the retinal image would be. This can be achieved by optical means, so that the image on the retina really is "upside down". Remember that the normal retinal image is upside down, according to our conventional reckoning of orientation with respect to gravity (Figure 2). Stratton's manipulation reversed this, so we can say that the retinal

15

image, although in one sense now "upright", was nevertheless opposite to what we normally experience. The immediate effect of the reversal is to make the visual world appear inverted, perhaps not surprisingly, as we know that there is at least an approximate map of the retinal surface in its cortical representation. What is quite amazing is the extent to which the human observer can adapt to this major distortion of visual appearances. Stratton wore the reversing spectacles for periods of several days, and his descriptions of the course of changes in how he perceived the world are fascinating (Stratton 1897). At first the disruption was great; he would bump into furniture, see his hands and feet in the "wrong" places, and move in the wrong directions. It would be difficult to point to objects, pick them up, and so on. Yet over the course of days many of these anomalies disappeared. The world never seemed quite normal, to be sure, but his success in adapting to it was incontrovertible. On removing the devices (having been careful to allow no "normal" vision during their use) a reverse distortion appeared in the normal world, to which re-adaptation had to occur.

Over the years many other psychologists have repeated experiments similar to Stratton's (Dolezal, 1982; Kohler, 1964) sometimes with much less radical distortions than his. It has been found that adaptation to "mild" distortions, ones for instance in which the retinal image is simply displaced and/or stretched, rather than being inverted, can occur quite rapidly and be essentially complete. Debate has raged about whether these adaptations are true visual effects, some theorists believing that the adaptations occur in the felt position of the head and limbs, for example, rather than in the visual representation itself. Interestingly enough, we can here see another facet of the nativist–empiricist division in perceptual psychology. Nativists tend to insist, given the well-established anatomical connections between retina and cortex, that nothing as feeble as a behavioural manipulation would be capable of affecting the transfer of information from one to the other (the "telephone switchboard" theory of visual function). For them, it is much easier to conceive of the plasticity as occurring in other modalities such as "felt limb position" or touch. Empiricists, on the other hand, have no such difficulty. Indeed plasticity, even at the physiological level, has now been demonstrated so convincingly that there is no a priori reason to deny its function in the visual representation. Further details on this debate can be found in Dodwell (1992). It may be mentioned that plasticity, or adaptability, is demonstrated in everyday life in the experience of people who wear corrective glasses. These change the sharpness with which images are projected on the retina, but also distort, to a greater or less degree, other characteristics, such as size and apparent distance. Yet virtually everyone, after an initial period of adjustment, is able to wear them and to adapt perfectly to the visual world.

THE NATURE OF PERCEPTUAL LEARNING

Unlike the Gestalt psychologists, Gibson did not deny that perceptual learning has a role to play in the production of a mature organism. Rather, he maintained that the nature of this learning is quite different from what the traditional empiricist account tells us. That account says that perceptual elements — cues — are atomistic, local, and in themselves essentially meaningless. Memory, habit, inference, and insight supply what is missing to construct the meaningful world. According to Gibson, the environment (the optic array in the first instance) supplies us with a much richer and more usable source of information; in fact in his view all the information needed to know and live in the world we normally inhabit. Perceptual learning, according to him, consists not in the gluing together of sensory "atoms", but in coming to differentiate and discriminate among the features of the environment, represented in the optic array. Indeed in his last major work, on "ecological optics", he maintained that virtually all cognitive activity could be analysed into components of discrimination within that array (Gibson, 1979).

Where's the truth? To most psychologists and philosophers of mind it seems inherently unlikely that one can understand cognition, of which perception is but the "front end", without resort to concepts that reach beyond the ground of "ecological validity" (Fodor & Pylyshyn, 1988). At the same time this is not to deny the importance of higher, more global concepts of stimulus attributes than the traditional theory allowed. It does not seem unreasonable to suggest that there are two different sorts of perceptual learning, one constructive, or synthetic, and another that, while not "destructive", is analytic in the Gibsonian sense. Synthetic perceptual learning might well be needed to account for the infant's ability to coordinate sights and sounds in forming concepts of *object permanency*, long held to be a constructive activity, whereas analytic processes might be involved in learning to discriminate between the faces of two distinct adults in the infant's environment. In the adult world a form of synthetic activity must be involved in learning the categories of *stamen* and *pistil*, for example, botanical categories defined much more by their functional attributes than by perceived characteristics. A more analytic form of discrimination learning, on the other hand, would be involved in learning to tell the difference between two shades of red, say *carmine* and *crimson*, or the difference between two vintages of wine (a favourite example of Gibson's). There is no good reason to restrict the number of different types of perceptual learning that are theoretically possible. If the study of perception has taught us anything, it is that a narrow focus on one point of view, valuable as it may be in furthering theory, runs the risk of distorting the truth.

BINOCULAR VISION AND DEPTH PERCEPTION

A remarkable fact about the normal visual system is that we have two eyes, each of which performs well on its own, but which function together to produce single visual images to which, as is easily shown, both eyes contribute. A look at the binocular system provides a suitable end-piece to this brief account of basic processes in vision, supplying as it does variations on most of the themes we have touched on.

At the centre of each retina is a small patch densely furnished with receptor cells which is called the *fovea*. It is the patch that is stimulated by that point in the visual field on which we fixate, and is mainly concerned with the detection of fine detail (and colour, but that is another story). The two eyes are independently mobile in their sockets, but by a near-automatic mechanism will converge in their lines of sight so that the same point is fixated by both (except in those unusual experimental situations in which psychologists cause different features to be presented to the two eyes). When properly fixated at some specific distance, we say that *corresponding points* in the two eyes are stimulated by features in the world that are at the same distance away as the fixation point. Objects nearer or farther therefore stimulate *non*-corresponding points, and it is a remarkable fact that in that case, the non-correspondence, provided it is not too great, gives rise to a totally new visual quality known as *stereoscopic* depth. Everyone will have seen this quality in the commercial stereoscopes so beloved of the Victorian era and still to be found as "Viewmasters" and the like. These involve the separate presentation to the two eyes of slightly different pictures (the two halves of a *stereogram*) which simulate the disparities present in real left and right-eye views of a scene.

What is the physiological basis for stereodepth perception? It was mentioned earlier that Hubel and Wiesel found most cells in the visual cortex to be binocularly driven. In their work it was assumed that the receptive fields in the two eyes were stimulating corresponding points in the two retinas. Yet it did not take long for Barlow and others to show, in the cat and subsequently in other mammals, that those binocular neurons can be divided into different classes, according to whether and by how much their "preferred" receptive fields are in non-corresponding parts of the two retinas (Barlow, Blakemore, & Pettigrew, 1967). The non-correspondence of the left and right eye retinal receptive fields are related to the distance at which "preferred" features are located. So we have here the physiological basis for coding stereodepth in the activity of single neurons.

That, in a sense, is only the beginning of the matter. Extensive research with humans has revealed a large and interesting field of inquiry with many puzzling and unexpected features. For example, how is it that we have two retinal images, but one visual world? What role does learning play in the production of stereoscopic depth effects? We know that there are many

18

different cues to depth, such as perspective, texture gradient, relative size, and interposition (one object nearer than another can obscure a part of it), and it seems these are subject to learning at least to some extent — *pace* Gibson. Yet it has been found that "pure stereoscopic depth" can be produced where there is no possibility of learning or interpretation playing a role. Stereograms have been designed in such a way that each half, that is to say the field presented to each separate eye, contains no regular pattern information and appears random, yet when the two halves are fused together a "binocular image" stands out from the fused background. These stereograms were first studied by the Hungarian-American psychologist Bela Julesz, and have led to the conclusion, supported by the physiological work described above, that there is an elementary stereo-detection code built into the mammalian visual system, just like the colour and contour coding systems described earlier (Julesz, 1971).

There are still many puzzling things about fused single vision. Is there genuine fusion of the images in the two eyes, or does one eye's image *suppress* the other? There is evidence for both processes! Hold your right thumb up about 30 cm from your nose, and fixate it carefully, so you see it as a single thumb (i.e., fused). Now hold up your left thumb behind the right one, at about 60 cm, carefully maintaining fixation on the near one. What do you see? Two sort of "ghost" thumbs, one to the right and one to the left of the near (fused) thumb (Figure 10). By alternately closing the left and right eyes you will be able to convince yourself that the ghost on the left is due to stimulation of the left eye, and that on the right comes from the right eye. If you are really careful, you can now fixate on the far thumb, and again you will see the two ghosts, but this time the right ghost is in the left eye, and conversely. These are called uncrossed and crossed disparity images respectively.

What are the ghosts? they are partially suppressed images of the full left and right eye images. Normally these are completely suppressed and we notice only the single, fused binocular images. If you think about it, your visual field must be full of such suppressed images, of which you are usually completely unaware. So suppression is a fact, fusion is a fact, the likely physiological basis for it is known, and the marvellous integration of the two processes allows us to see unconfabulated images, with the additional advantage of a new and reliable cue to depth.

As was mentioned, there are many other cues to depth and distance, most of which can override stereodepth. For example if you reverse the two parts of a stereogram in a stereoscope, so the right eye sees the left eye's view and vice versa, you will still see good depth if the scene depicted is of a rich natural scene like a landscape or building. Here *interpretation* clearly takes precedence over the built-in processing system for stereodepth which, on its own, should produce reversed depth impressions.

So, binocular vision and depth perception show in miniature, as it were, many of the characteristics of visual perception as a whole; we know

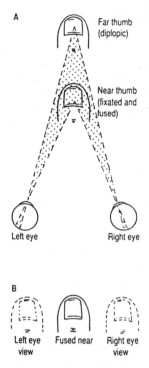

Figure 10   The fused view of the near thumb, and the two "ghost" images to the left and right (see text for further explanation)

something of the physiological substrate, its phenomenology tells us important things about what is going on (suppression and fusion, for example), and it even supplies evidence of how important experience and interpretation can be in reaching a coherent and seamless view of the perceptual world.

CONCLUSION

The wide scope of research in perception, the ways it can aid us in understanding the intricacies of the perceptual apparatus, how it is used to inform us about the world, and how it is "tuned up" in the course of development have been our main themes. I have also tried to give some idea of the flavour of modern theorizing in the psychology of perception, for it is after all this which guides us in our attempts to understand both the apparatus and its function. If the emphasis has seemed at times to be heavily on the physiological side, this is because advances in understanding of the physiological substrate of vision have been so impressive since the 1950s. Yet I would be the last to argue that all we need to know about perception is exhausted by this knowledge, and I hope that has come through in my account too.

Nativism and empiricism still are the primary poles in the theoretical dialogue about the nature of perception. They seem to be in some way quite intractable, and are most unlikely to go away. This is not because they do not involve factual differences which can be settled by experimentation. Such differences exist of course, but the debate between the two poles is largely theoretical if not metaphysical, and reflects a difference in the predilection of individual scientists for accounting for perceptual phenomena on one basis or another. From that point of view we are not much further ahead than were Helmholtz and Hering in the 1880s, even though our store of detailed knowledge about the visual system and about perception is now vastly greater than theirs.

What are the primary problems that await solution in the psychology of perception? One without doubt is the question of the "seamless web" of perceptual experience (Dodwell, 1992). We have plenty of ideas and information about the processing of visual information, especially as this is evinced in the activity of single cells in the visual system, but not too many yet about its integration into the meaningful objects and events of our normal cognitive world. Some powerful ideas come from the recent field of computational vision; readers will have to decide for themselves how successful this enterprise is in that regard. Another primary question has to do with the fitting of our internal representation of the world to the external reality (Andrews, 1964). I have not said much about this, as it is an area of research still in its infancy, but one which no doubt will grow in time to match its importance as an epistemological problem (Dodwell & Humphrey, 1990).

What is that problem? We know much about the transduction of physical energy into neural signals, quite a bit about how these are transmitted to the brain, yet almost nothing about how the signals come to represent reality, as surely they must. Is this an empirical problem capable of scientific resolution? In some respects it certainly is, but nothing I have written about, for instance, will account for the fact that straight lines look straight. Indeed much of what we know about sensory coding seems to suggest that "straightness" is quite foreign to the operation of the physiological system. Many cells "prefer" short line segments, but how these are integrated into the global contours of the visual field is not accounted for by that fact. Mathematical modelling, involving integration of these line elements in "vector fields" may supply the answer (Hoffman, 1966; Hoffman & Dodwell, 1985). Yet there it is; straight lines look straight, and this is especially puzzling because if we put on a distorting lens (even an ordinary spectacle lens) that causes the line to look bent, we adapt pretty soon, so that it again looks straight! This is basically the same puzzle that beset the Gestalt psychologist Koffka in the 1930s. He asked "Why does a tree look like a tree?" (Koffka, 1935). One might say that this is too broad and general a question to be answered scientifically, like the question "What is life?" But, like that question, ours is too urgent to be neglected. Gibson had his answer (it is all in the optical array; no other sources of information are relevant). The empiricists, following Berkeley and Helmholtz, had their answer too (it is all in the mind, depending on the individual's experiences of the world), and other psychologists have made similarly sweeping pronouncements. I hope that I have been able to show that all such answers are too simple. Perception is a many-faceted beast, and answers to its many problems need to be sought in different places, and at different levels of function; sensory, organizational, cognitive. This is the reason why the study of perception is so rich and rewarding. We can be sure that it will continue to pose puzzles to the researcher for the foreseeable future. To perceive seems effortless. To understand perception is nevertheless a great challenge.

FURTHER READING

Dodwell, P. C. (1990). *Perception*. In R. Lockhart, J. Grusec, & J. Waller (Eds) *Foundations of perception* (chap. 5). Toronto: Copp Clark Pitman.
Gregory, R. L. (1966). *Eye and brain*. New York: McGraw-Hill.
Hubel, D. H. (1987). *Eye, brain and vision*. New York: Freeman.
Rock, I. (1984). *Perception*. New York: Scientific American.
Schiffman, H. R. (1982). *Sensation and perception: An integrated approach* (2nd edn). New York: Wiley.

REFERENCES

Andrews, D. P. (1964). Error-correcting perceptual mechanisms. *Quarterly Journal of Experimental Psychology*, *16*, 104–115.
Banks, W. P., & Krajicek, D. (1991). Perception. *Annual Review of Psychology*, *42*, 305–331.
Barlow, H. B., Blakemore, C., & Pettigrew, J. O. (1967). The neural mechanism of binocular depth discrimination. *Journal of Physiology*, *193*, 327–342.
Blakemore, C. (1978). Maturation and modification in the developing visual system. In R. Held, H. Liebowitz, & H. Teuber (Eds) *Handbook of sensory physiology: Perception* (vol. 8., pp. 377–436). New York: Springer.
Boring, E. (1950). *A history of experimental psychology*. New York: Appleton-Century-Crofts.
Cronly-Dillon, J. R. (Ed.) (1991). *Vision and visual dysfunction* (general ed. J. R. Cronly-Dillon): *vol. 11. Development and plasticity in the visual system*. London: Macmillan.
Cutting, J. E. (1987). Perception and information. *Annual Review of Psychology*, *38*, 61–90.
Dodwell, P. C. (1970). *Visual pattern recognition*. New York: Holt, Rinehart & Winston.
Dodwell, P. C. (1992). Perspectives and transformations. *Canadian Journal of Psychology*, *46*, 510–538.
Dodwell, P. C., & Humphrey, G. K. (1990). A functional theory of the McCollough effect. *Psychological Review*, *97*, 78–89.
Dolezal, H. (1982). *Living in a world transformed*. New York: Academic Press.

Dreher, B., & Robinson, S. R. (Eds) (1991). *Vision and visual dysfunction* (general ed. J. R. Cronly-Dillon): *vol. 3. Neuroanatomy of the visual pathways and their development*. London: Macmillan.

Fodor, J. A., & Pylyshyn, Z. W. (1988). Connectionism and cognitive architecture. *Cognition, 89*, 3–71.

Gibson, E. J. (1988). Exploratory behaviour in the development of perceiving, acting and acquiring of knowledge. *Annual Review of Psychology, 39*, 1–41.

Gibson, J. J. (1950). *The perception of the visual world*. Boston, MA: Houghton Mifflin.

Gibson, J. J. (1966). *The senses considered as perceptual systems*. Boston, MA: Houghton Mifflin.

Gibson, J. J. (1979). *The ecological approach to visual perception*. Boston, MA: Houghton Mifflin.

Hebb, D. O. (1949). *The organization of behavior*. New York: Wiley.

Held, R. (1965) Plasticity in sensorimotor systems. *Scientific American, 213*(5), 84–94.

Hoffman, W. C. (1966). The Lie algebra of visual perception. *Journal of Mathematical Psychology, 3*, 65–98.

Hoffman, W. C., & Dodwell, P. C. (1985). Geometric psychology generates the visual gestalt. *Canadian Journal of Psychology, 39*, 491–528.

Hubel, D. H., & Wiesel, T. N. (1962). Receptive fields, binocular interaction and functional architecture in the cat's visual cortex. *Journal of Physiology, 160*, 106–115.

Julesz, B. (1971). *Foundations of cyclopean perception*. Chicago, IL: Chicago University Press.

Kilpatrick, F. P. (1961). *Explorations in transactional psychology*. New York: New York University Press.

Koffka, K. (1935). *The principles of Gestalt psychology*. New York: Harcourt Brace & World.

Kohler, I. (1964). The formation and transformation of the perceptual world. *Psychological Issues, 3*, 1–173 (original German, 1951).

Köhler, W. (1929). *Gestalt psychology*. New York: Liveright.

Kubovy, M., & Pomerantz, J. R. (Eds) (1981). *Perceptual organization*. Hillsdale, NJ: Lawrence Erlbaum.

Maunsell, J. H. R., & Newsome, W. T. (1987). Visual processing in monkey extrastriate cortex. *Annual Review of Neuroscience, 10*, 363–401.

Perrett, D. I., Smith, P. A. J., Potter, D. D., Mistlin, A. J., Head, A. S., Milner, A. D., & Jeeves, M. A. (1985). Visual cells in the temporal cortex sensitive to face view and gaze direction. *Proceedings of the Royal Society of London, B, 223*, 293–317.

Rock, I. (1984). *Perception*. New York: Scientific American.

Stratton, G. M. (1897). Vision without inversion of the retinal image. *Psychological Review, 4*, 341–360; 463–481.

Wallach, H. (1987). Perceiving a stable environment when one moves. *Annual Review of Psychology, 38*, 1–27.

2

COMPUTATIONAL THEORIES OF VISION

Mike G. Harris and Glyn W. Humphreys
University of Birmingham, England

Imagine a pond surrounded by children throwing stones into the water. As each stone lands, it creates an expanding pattern of ripples on the surface. Sometimes several stones land at the same time, so that the surface is thrown into a complex, ever-changing pattern. Now consider the problems of working out how big each stone was and where it landed in the pond, given the seemingly artificial constraints that you cannot see or hear and that your only contact with the world is through your two index fingers, which you are allowed to dip into water to feel the ripples drifting by.

This simple scene offers a fairly direct analogy with hearing and, more generally, with senses such as vision, where information about the world is conveyed indirectly to the perceiver. The point is that to solve the problems set by the analogy, and more importantly to understand a good solution, you would need to know about the relationships between stones and ripples and about how they are represented in the patterns arriving at your fingertips. You would also need to be very specific about the kinds of information you are trying to extract. Information in the above context means those aspects of the ripples that are useful to a specific task: if you were interested in the size of the stones it might be the size of the ripples, but if you were interested in where they landed it might be the difference in the time of arrival of a particular ripple at the two fingers. These two ingredients – an understanding of the relationships between the stimulus and the object that produced it, and a proper specification of the problem that you are trying to solve – form the essential basis of a computational theory, which is simply a principled description of those aspects of the stimulus that are potentially useful to completing a specified task. The thrust of a computational theory is thus not just to explain *how* things work, but *why* they work the way they do.

A computational theory is an abstract description of the relationships between world, stimulus and task. It is the first, and most important, step in understanding some aspect of perception but it is not, by itself, enough. Having identified the aspects of the stimulus that are important to a particular task we must also think about how these aspects might be extracted, represented, and processed, and about how each stage might actually be carried out. These additional steps are generally important because a given computational theory may suggest several different ways to proceed. To psychologists, the additional steps are absolutely essential because psychologists are interested not only in how a problem *might* be solved, but also in how it *is* solved within the brain. A computational theory can identify only the theoretical constraints on what is possible and, to take into account the biological constraints on what is practicable, we must use it to derive a specific representation and a neurally plausible implementation.

Since a computational theory is just an abstract description, it has nothing inherently to do with computers and, in that sense, the name is unfortunate. However, even more confusingly, computational theories almost invariably lead to working computer models and the models and the theories together make up the computational approach to vision. Working computer models obviously provide a rigorous test of a particular implementation but they also have another important role, which follows indirectly from the fact that we cannot hope to develop a single computational theory of vision, because vision is not a single task. Vision is like a service industry which contributes to a broad range of behaviours including, among others, navigation, balance, object recognition, and the guidance of social interaction. Each of these different types of behaviours consists of many tasks, each requiring its own computational theory, so that the computational approach is inevitably very modular. If we are to gain a full understanding of vision rather than just its

25

parts, we must also have an overall framework that specifies the interactions between the modules. The development of large-scale computer models, which combine several modules in the simulation of substantial aspects of perception, is thus an essential adjunct of the computational approach.

MARR'S COMPUTATIONAL FRAMEWORK FOR OBJECT RECOGNITION

Since a general overview of computational theories would inevitably be very superficial, this chapter concentrates upon the single theme of object recognition, outlining some of the recent developments in this one important area. Rather than following an historical sequence, the material is structured around the framework developed by the late David Marr (Marr, 1982), who first popularized the computational approach, and whose framework (outlined in Figure 1) remains the widest ranging computational account of visual object recognition.

Marr's framework starts from the idea that such useful attributes of a three-dimensional (3D) scene as surface markings, object boundaries, and

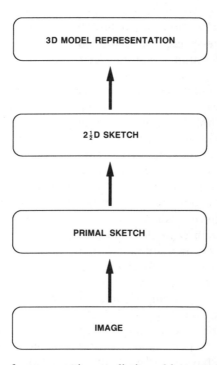

Figure 1 The levels of representation mediating object recognition, proposed by Marr (1982)

shadows can all be recovered from the basic retinal input by locating and describing the places where the intensity of the image changes relatively abruptly from place to place. He argued that these properties could be captured in something he termed a primal sketch. Two stages of deriving the primal sketch were distinguished. The raw primal sketch involves coding and locating individual intensity changes within a map based on the retina. The full primal sketch involves a more elaborate description in which the individual edge fragments are grouped into more meaningful clusters relating to surfaces. At the next stage, information about the distance and layout of each surface were added using a variety of techniques, or "depth cues". The resulting representation is termed the $2\frac{1}{2}$D sketch because it describes only the *visible* parts of the scene and is thus not fully three-dimensional. The $2\frac{1}{2}$D sketch will not serve for object recognition, however, because this requires that the input representation of the object be mapped against a representation stored in memory. Since the $2\frac{1}{2}$D sketch changes with the observer's viewpoint, it could be matched with memory only if representations were stored for all encountered views. To lessen the memory requirements of this process, Marr suggested that a further representation be constructed, which he termed a 3D model description. In this representation the parts of objects are coded relative to some salient part of the object itself, so that the resultant description remains the same across different views.

This framework is obviously "bottom-up" in nature, being concerned primarily with how information is extracted and built up into useful descriptions from the basic retinal input. Thus, the early stages of the framework make only very general assumptions about the structure of the external world, and do not call upon knowledge about specific objects. This contrasts sharply with the alternative "top-down" approach, where knowledge about specific objects or scenes can be used to facilitate, or even bypass, some of the earlier descriptive stages. While a bottom-up framework is not an inevitable consequence of the computational approach, it has certainly dominated recent research, at least partly because it is easier to derive computational theories for the early stages of perception where the relationships between the stimulus and the world are much easier to specify.

THE RAW PRIMAL SKETCH

Edge detection

The Marr and Hildreth (1980) account of edge detection is one of the earliest computational theories and is worth considering in some detail as an excellent example of the computational approach. When asked to sketch an object, most people begin with a simple line drawing rather than by shading in solid regions of colour. This is reasonable because the line drawing emphasizes two useful kinds of edge—object boundaries, which economically convey the

27

object's overall shape, and the edges delineating the position and shape of detailed features and surface markings. Faced with the problem of recognizing, rather than depicting, an object, we can apply the logic in reverse and begin with a description based on edges. In general, these will appear in an image as places where the luminance changes fairly abruptly from place to place. Such changes are called luminance discontinuities. Of course, a description of these discontinuities is by no means complete because not all edges will produce discontinuities – some will, for example, be occluded – and not all discontinuities will correspond to real features of the object – some will, for example, correspond to shadows. The second of these problems, at least, can be solved by breaking the task into two stages: first locating and describing the luminance discontinuities in the image, then deciding which of them correspond to object features. The better the description produced in the first stage, the easier the second stage will be. For example, shadows tend to produce relative broad luminance discontinuities, so they can be distinguished from edges if the steepness of the change is known.

The detection of luminance discontinuities

The best way to find luminance discontinuities is simply to subtract the amount of light at one point in the image from that at adjacent points because, by definition, this subtraction will give a non-zero result in the presence of a luminance discontinuity. This process is known technically as spatial differentiation. However, there are three complications to be overcome:

1 Because luminance discontinuities occur at different spatial scales (sharp or gradual) and because no single scale of comparison can detect them all, several comparisons need to be made simultaneously at a range of different scales.
2 Because discontinuities can occur at any orientation, comparisons need to be made simultaneously at all orientations.
3 Images are inherently "noisy" so that, even under perfect viewing conditions, luminance varies randomly from place to place. Spatial differentiation is very sensitive to this noise and will tend to signal many spurious luminance discontinuities. To avoid this, the image must be "smoothed" by calculating the *average* luminance over a small area before making the comparison. The exact size of the area is crucial because averaging over a large area will blur out the discontinuities, while averaging over a small area won't reduce the noise. The best compromise is to calculate a *weighted* average – so that the luminance near the point of interest contributes a lot to the average, and more remote points contribute relatively

little. The ideal weighting function is the Gaussian (or Normal) distribution, familiar in statistics, since it averages over a wide area but assigns most of the weight to a small region near the centre.

As shown in Figure 2, the receptive field of a typical retinal ganglion cell (the type of cell that signals the result of retinal processing to higher visual centres) seems to embody all these requirements. The two sub-regions average the light over adjacent areas of the image, the antagonistic arrangement of the sub-regions takes the difference between these averages, and the circular shape ensures that the comparisons are made at all orientations. At each point on the retina, there are retinal ganglion cells with different sized receptive fields, so that the comparisons are done simultaneously at a range of spatial scales.

According to Marr and Hildreth's computational theory, retinal processes have evolved to emphasize luminance discontinuities – a task that requires Gaussian smoothing followed by spatial differentiation. An individual retinal ganglion cell performs these operations at one point in the image and an array of similar cells, one at each point, analyses the whole image. At a more technical level, the analysis predicts the precise form of the receptive field profile shown in Figure 2b, and psychophysical studies of human observers (e.g., Wilson & Bergen, 1979) confirm that the mechanisms underlying edge detection have sensitivity profiles which are very close approximations to this prediction.

The position of luminance discontinuities is normally given by the position of "zero-crossings" in the description resulting from smoothing and differentiation (Figure 2c), so that the problem of detecting edges becomes the problem of detecting zero-crossings. Zero-crossings can be detected in a biologically plausible way by wiring together groups of retinal ganglion cells in the manner shown in Figure 3. Cells with on- and off-centre receptive fields forming two adjacent, parallel rows are connected by a logical "AND" so that an output occurs only when both rows are simultaneously responding positively, a situation that generally occurs only in the presence of an appropriately oriented zero-crossing. The resulting device – a model of the "simple" cells which form the first stage of processing in the visual cortex – would thus function as an "oriented zero-crossing detector". Individual simple cells do indeed have the required oriented receptive fields and, for each retinal position, there are many simple cells with receptive fields covering the full range of orientations (Hubel & Wiesel, 1962, 1968) and spatial scales (Tootell, Silverman, & De Valois, 1981).

Making edge assertions

The result of these processes is a set of zero-crossing maps of the image, each depicting a different spatial scale. The final stage of the analysis is to convert

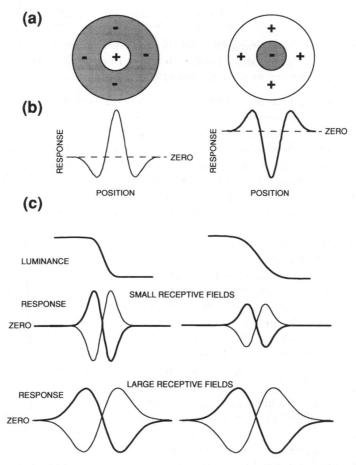

Figure 2 (a) The receptive field of typical retinal ganglion cells. A microelectrode is placed in or close to a cell and its response is monitored while a small spot of light is moved about the retina. The receptive field is the area of the retina in which the light causes a change in the cell's response. Under diffuse lighting conditions, retinal ganglion cells have a spontaneous background firing rate. A small spot of light may cause an increase (excitatory, indicated by a +) or a decrease (inhibitory, indicated by a −) in response, depending on its position within the receptive field. The example on the left is an "on-centre" cell, in which the central sub-region is excitatory. That on the right is an "off-centre" cell. An equal number of both types is found in the retina. (b) The receptive field sensitivity profiles of the cells in (a), indicating the precise sensitivity of the cell to light at each position in the receptive field. The profile shown is that predicted by Marr's analysis and is known mathematically as $\nabla^2 G$ (del-squared G). It is produced by differentiating a Gaussian function twice and (in the case of the on-centre cell) inverting the result. (The second differentiation is needed so that spatial comparisons are performed at all orientations.) (c) The pattern of response in an array of retinal ganglion cells to luminance discontinuities at different spatial scales. Two different sizes of receptive field are shown, corresponding to $\nabla^2 G$ derived from Gaussian functions of two different widths (standard deviations). The bolder line represents the response of on-centre cells, the finer line that of off-centre cells

30

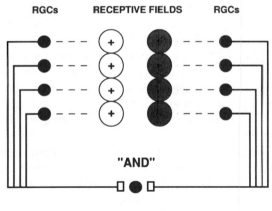

Figure 3 Marr's model of a cortical simple cell as an "oriented zero-crossing detector". Two sets of retinal ganglion cells (RGCs), one consisting of on-centre cells and the other of off-centre cells, with suitably positioned receptive fields are wired together by a logical "AND". The resulting simple cell responds only when *both* sets of RGCs are active. For clarity, only the centre sub-regions of the receptive fields are shown

this complex description of the image into a single, symbolic description which captures the layout of object features in the world. Unlike noise, real object features will tend to produce zero-crossings at more than one spatial scale, and so "edge assertions" are made only where the zero-crossing maps coincide. Each edge assertion can then be described in terms of its position, contrast, orientation, scale, and so forth, by analysing the pattern of response across the different maps. For example, it is clear from Figure 2c, that the pattern of response at different spatial scales conveys information about the slope of the edge.

It is important to recognize that the final result of all this processing – the raw primal sketch – is a list of *symbols* which make assertions about the external world and which can be conveniently manipulated by further processes. It thus has a very different status from the simple, zero-crossing maps which only describe the image. In Marr's original framework, the raw primal sketch is the basis for all subsequent analysis, and higher level processes have no access to the zero-crossing maps on which it is based.

Comments, criticisms, and extensions

On the face of it, the computational theory that underpins the above account of edge detection is a simple statement about the descriptive usefulness of luminance discontinuities. At a deeper level, however, the entire analysis is driven by the proper understanding of the relationships between edges and images that the computational theory requires. Thus, the theory leads directly to the constraints that emphasize smoothing and differentiation and to the processes that distinguish edges from random noise. Indeed, precisely the same computational theory underpins the edge detection routines that are currently popular in computer vision (e.g., Canny, 1986) though here, because biological constraints are unimportant, the final representation and implementation is rather different. From a psychological viewpoint, the theory describes the *why*, as well as *how*, of visual processing and should be compared with earlier accounts of simple cells as "feature detectors" (e.g., Hubel & Wiesel, 1962) which, lacking any computational theory, assigned far too much responsibility to the responses of individual cells.

The account so far deals only with static images and thus takes no account of the information provided by the smooth transformations, or flow patterns, which accompany movement of the observer through the world (see, for example, Gibson, 1979). This information could, in principle, be recovered later by analysing the changes in a sequence of raw primal sketches (Ullman, 1979) but there are also several computational accounts of how motion can be extracted directly from the image (Adelson & Movshon, 1982; Heeger, 1987; Marr & Ullman, 1981). Marr and Ullman's account, for example, emphasizes the role of temporal differentiation (comparisons over time, rather than across position) and leads directly to an implementation requiring only a small refinement of the scheme outlined above. Although the original computational theory deals only with motion direction, it can easily be extended to encompass speed (Harris, 1986), leading to a *dynamic* raw primal sketch in which each edge assertion includes a description of its image velocity.

More serious criticisms of Marr and Hildreth's model begin with the details of the implementation. Neurophysiological studies (Robson, 1980) show that the receptive fields of retinal ganglion cells do not have precisely the form illustrated in Figure 2b, but that this property is more compatible with cortical mechanisms, which have elongated receptive fields and are thus already selective for stimulus orientation (Hawken & Parker, 1987). More importantly, although cortical simple cells do combine the outputs of several retinal ganglion cells, there is little evidence of the logical AND operation which is so important to Marr's way of making edge assertion (Hochstein & Spitzer, 1984). In general, while retaining the basic notions of smoothing and differentiation, recent accounts have provided alternative accounts of subsequent processing (e.g., Watson & Ahumada 1989; Watt & Morgan, 1985). To take a specific example, Watt and Morgan point out that the positions of zero-crossings can be misleading in noisy images and argue instead for more reliable descriptions based on the position and size of the peaks and troughs in the response patterns shown in Figure 2c. Originally, these descriptive primitives were used only to derive edge assertions like those of Marr but

32

Watt (1991) developed a rather more general computational theory based on the simple principle that rare events are the most informative. This leads to a process of statistical image description in which the mean and standard deviation (i.e., variability) of some image property are calculated, and only those features that have significantly unusual properties contribute to the final description. According to this more general view, the peaks and troughs in Figure 2c are simply rare responses which are consequently selected for further processing.

THE FULL PRIMAL SKETCH

All computational theories of early visual processing begin with an initial description which, like the raw primal sketch, emphasizes localized variations in image luminance. The same principle seems to apply within the visual system in that all retinal and most cortical cells have localized receptive fields so that each processes only a small region of the image. The resulting computational or neural representation is therefore very fragmentary, rather like a partly solved jigsaw in which the individual pieces preserve the informative features of the image but fail to capture the meaningful structure of the scene in terms of surfaces and objects.

The computational theory behind the recovery of this large-scale structure, as proposed by Marr, is based on two very simple but very powerful constraints. First, matter is coherent so that symbols that are close together in the image will usually belong to the same object. Second, symbols that share a common descriptive attribute will usually have a common physical cause. So, for example, symbols sharing similar orientations might first be grouped together to form larger-scale symbols with new descriptive attributes such as shape and texture, and the process might then be repeated upon these new symbols. Such simple and powerful grouping not only reveals additional image properties, such as texture gradients which are potentially useful in inferring depth (see below), but it also allows the recognition of additional object boundaries as places where the new image property changes abruptly from place to place.

Comments, criticisms, and extensions

The full primal sketch provides a functional explanation for the perceptual grouping strategies illustrated in Figure 4, which were extensively studied by the Gestalt psychologists (e.g., Wertheimer, 1912). On the basis of demonstrations such as those illustrated in Figure 4, the Gestalt psychologists drew up a set of principles of grouping, stating that (for instance) items tend to group if they are close to one another (the law of proximity), are similar (the law of similarity), make a good form, continue a single edge (good continuation), have a common pattern of motion (common fate). These

33

demonstrations provided a comprehensive description of the rules by which human observers cluster individual stimulus elements into coherent structures but, because they were confined to artificial stimuli and laboratory phenomena, say nothing about why grouping is a *necessary* perceptual stage. Of course, within any account such as Marr's, grouping is a necessary process because edge descriptions will be fragmentary. Grouping also helps the visual system to deal with incomplete data and with complex scenes, where the images of different objects may occlude each other. For example, grouping two edges by good continuation enables the visual system to register the presence of a single large object when a smaller object is placed in front of it.

Early attempts to develop computer vision systems, prior to Marr's work,

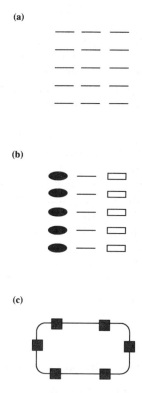

Figure 4 Examples of Gestalt properties of proximity (a), similarity (b), and good continuation (c). In (a) horizontal lines tend to be seen rather than vertical lines, because the elements in the horizontal lines are closer together. In (b) vertical lines tend to be seen, even though the vertical elements are further apart from the horizontal elements, because the vertically aligned elements are identical while the horizontally aligned elements differ. Thus the vertical elements group more strongly by similarity. In (c) the background oblong is seen beneath the smaller squares because the broken contour of the oblong can be grouped by good continuation

also paid considerable attention to grouping phenomena, and attempted to implement grouping procedures in terms of simple interactions between edges and junctions in shapes. These attempts, epitomized in the work on the so-called "blocks world", involved the development of programs to segment displays comprising a fixed set of object types (cylinders, wedges, pyramids, and so forth), on the basis of simple rules governing the relations between the lines in the images (e.g., Clowes, 1971; Guzman, 1968). This work was limited, in that it used highly simplified representations of the world, and so failed to confront the many problems encountered with real images. It also tended to adopt solutions specific to its own limited domain, rather than developing more general-purpose algorithms that serve across different domains.

Marr's account, with its emphasis of the computational constraints involved both in coding edges and subsequently in grouping edges together, provides a richer description of the input, and this is necessary if robust and generalizable procedures are to be developed (across different contrasts, scale, and so forth). More recently, Watt's (1991) account, computing statistical summaries at each stage of description and identifying unusual elements for the next stage, also offers a promising, and more general, refinement of the theory.

Marr's account of how the full primal sketch is derived emphasizes that grouping takes place within a two-dimensional representation, coded in retinal co-ordinates. Recent empirical research suggests that this is not the case, however, and that visual grouping processes may employ quite "deep" assumptions about the three-dimensional structure of the world. For instance, differences in the three-dimensional structure of block figures give rise to the instantaneous perception of an "odd-man-out", even when there are no two-dimensional orientation differences present (Enns & Rensink, 1990; see also Figure 5). This suggests rapid coding of the spatial relations

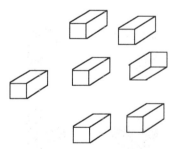

Figure 5 Example of rapid "pop out" of a block differing in its 3D orientation from the background, even though there are no 2D orientation differences present. This indicates that grouping and segmentation of the blocks is operating using 3D rather than 2D representations

between edges in three- rather than two-dimensions across the visual field. Also, by assuming that the world is three-dimensional, and that the corners of solid objects often form right angles, the three-dimensional structure of objects can be coded rapidly, with little other spatial information required (Perkins, 1968).

In contrast to our understanding of the neural mechanisms mediating the coding of the raw primal sketch, our understanding of the neural mechanisms involved in the full primal sketch is limited. Workers have shown that cells within area V2 of the cortex, an area taking input directly from the primary visual cortex, respond to the presence of an "illusory" contour between two co-linear edges (e.g., they respond to the illusory bar present in the Kanisza figure shown in Figure 6; Peterhans & von der Heydt, 1989). This suggests that cells in V2 play a role in grouping between co-linear edges coded at different retinal locations. Little is known about the ways in which neural mechanisms implement three-dimensional constraints on grouping.

One of the reasons for the relative sparsity of knowledge about the neurophysiological mechanisms mediating grouping is that, to date, neurophysiological studies have largely examined the response properties of single neurons whereas grouping probably involves interactions between neurons (e.g., two neurons in the primary visual cortex pooling their outputs into a common cell that responds to continuation between the lines activating the primary cortex neurons). Studies examining the properties of groups of neurons suggest that the time-locking of cell responses may be important in linking cells together in response to Gestalt properties in the environment (e.g., Gray & Singer, 1989). Such time-locking of responses may in turn impose constraints on visual grouping (e.g., it may limit the number of groups that can be maintained without interference). The exploration of the computational constraints thus imposed is only just beginning (e.g., Hummel & Biederman, 1992). One promising avenue for research here concerns attempts to implement processes dependent on the interaction between

Figure 6   A Kanisza square. An illusory contour is seen joining the pacmen together. Neurophysiological evidence indicates that such contours are computed as early as area V2 in the cortex

neurons within "connectionist" models. These models generate intelligent behaviour from interactions between large numbers of computationally simple processing units, which (for example) summate activity from their "input" cells and pass on either excitatory or inhibitory input to their "output" cells. Since it is the pattern of interaction within a network of such cells that underlies behaviour, such models may provide valid ways to capture grouping processes in vision. Attempts to simulate completion phenomena in V2 cells, for instance, have been made by Grossberg and his colleagues (e.g., Grossberg & Mingolla, 1985).

THE $2\frac{1}{2}$D SKETCH

One of the most difficult problems faced by any sophisticated visual system is the need to reconstruct a depthy description of the world from flat retinal images. The main contribution of psychologists to this area has been the identification of the many different types of information – termed depth cues – which are useful to this task, while, recently, the computational approach has provided more precise theories of how (and, of course, why) each of these cues is used. For example, computational theories now exist for the recovery of 3D shape, at least under certain conditions, from linear perspective (Clowes, 1971; Draper, 1981; Huffman, 1971; Kanade, 1981; Waltz, 1975), shading (Horn, 1977), texture (Blake & Marinos, 1990) and motion (Clocksin, 1980; Koenderink, 1986; Longuet-Higgins & Prazdny, 1980; Rieger & Lawton, 1985; Waxman & Wohn, 1988). Again, rather than considering each of these rather superficially, we shall concentrate upon just one important example, that of stereopsis (literally "solid vision").

Stereopsis relies upon the fact that we have two separate views of the world, one for each eye, taken from slightly different viewpoints. As you can readily confirm by opening and closing each eye alternately, these two views are slightly different – and these differences, called disparities, contain information about the distance of objects in the world. The analysis of stereopsis is, in principle, very simple: one simply compares the two images, detects and measures the disparities, and analyses the disparities to recover depth. A problem, however, arises at the first, comparison, stage. Provided the images have already been recognized, it is easy to compare the positions of some identifiable feature in the two images but, at least in a bottom-up framework, stereopsis is supposed to be an *aid* to recognition, rather than a consequence. In fact, many years ago Julesz (1971) demonstrated that stereopsis can occur prior to recognition using an elegant stimulus called the random dot stereogram. Each eye is presented separately with essentially the same pattern of randomly positioned dots, the only difference between them being that, in one image, a region of dots (say a square) is displaced slightly to one side. This introduces a disparity which human observers can detect, so that they experience a compelling impression of the displaced region standing out in

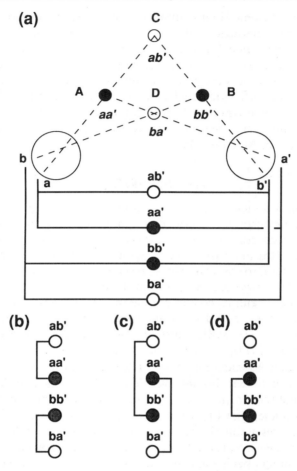

Figure 7 The correspondence problem. (a) Two objects (A and B) produce two images (a and b) in the left eye and two images (a' and b') in the right eye. When these images are correctly matched (*aa'* and *bb'*), the objects are seen in their correct positions. However, it is also possible to match the images incorrectly (*ab'* and *ba'*), in which case the objects are seen in incorrect positions (C and D). Binocular cells (ab', aa', bb', and ba') each combines one of the images from each of the eyes and thus make all possible matches (i.e., each cell responds because it has an appropriate stimulus in both of its receptive fields). (b)–(d) show the connections between the binocular cells needed to implement Marr and Poggio's (1976) solution to the correspondence problem. (b) *Only one object is visible along each line of sight* from the left eye, so *inhibitory* connections are made between aa' and ab', and between ba' and bb'. (c) The same rule for the right eye results in *inhibitory* connections between bb' and ab', and between ba' and aa'. (d) *Depth varies slowly*, so *excitatory* connections are made between aa' and bb', since they are in the same depth plane

depth from the background. Since the individual images are completely unstructured and contain no recognizable features, stereopsis can occur without prior recognition of the images.

Random dot stereograms emphasize the basic problem of stereopsis: since each image may contain several thousand dots, how does the visual system work out which dot in one image corresponds with which dot in the other? This is known as the correspondence problem. Getting the correspondence wrong (making a "false match"), as illustrated for a very simple case in Figure 7, is equivalent to seeing an object at the wrong position. Although the correspondence problem appears formidable, Marr and Poggio's (1976) computational theory argues that it can be solved by recognizing just two fundamental constraints. First, only one object can usually be seen at any one time along each line of sight, so that many potential correspondences are mutually incompatible. Second, objects generally have relatively smooth surfaces, so that distance will usually vary rather gradually from place to place. (Note that this is just the inverse of the familiar argument that object boundaries are rare and thus informative.)

These simple constraints translate almost directly into a recipe for solving the correspondence problem: first make all possible matches between the two images and then weaken those that are mutually incompatible while strengthening those that are likely to occur together. This recipe translates equally directly into the plausible neural implementation illustrated at the bottom of Figure 7. Binocular units — which receive input from both eyes — make all possible matches by responding whenever an appropriate feature occurs at the appropriate positions in both images. These units are interconnected by inhibitory and excitatory links which implement the second part of the recipe, so that units representing the same line of sight inhibit each other, while those representing the same distance, or "depth plane", excite each other. When the resulting neural network is presented with a random dot stereogram many units initially respond but, as the inhibitory and excitatory interconnections exert their influence, it rapidly settles down to a stable state in which only those units representing the correct 3D interpretation continue to respond.

Comments, criticisms, and extensions

The model outlined above is, in fact, a rather early attempt chosen for its clarity and because it provides a good example of a connectionist approach to a particular visual processing problem. More recent accounts (e.g., Marr & Poggio, 1979; Pollard, Mayhew, & Frisby, 1985) have considered whether correspondence matches should be based on the primal sketch or whether they should have access to the earlier zero-crossing maps so that matches can first be made at coarse spatial scales and then progressively refined. They have also introduced the concept of "disparity gradient", which is a convenient way to represent the way that distance in the world changes across position in the image and thus provides a convenient measure for the constraint on smoothness of depth variation. None the less, such developments can be viewed essentially as refinements of the same basic computational theory.

Work on the $2\frac{1}{2}$D sketch has by and large emphasized single processes (or modules) that provide depthy representations of stimuli – stereopsis being a prime example. It remains poorly understood how the different forms of input to such a representation might be combined, what the representation so formed might specify, and what purposes it might serve. Marr (1982) suggested that such a representation might be useful for action, since it would specify the relative depth of the surface of the object to the viewer. In this way, the $2\frac{1}{2}$D sketch would serve a different computational purpose from the 3D model description, which, being viewpoint invariant, cannot be used to guide actions directly, but which is useful for recognition. However, different input modules provide information suiting subtly different purposes. For example, stereopsis can provide accurate information about the relative distances of surfaces from an observer, but it is less suited to providing information about the tilt and slant of each point on the surface. In contrast, surface tilt and slant can be reliably provided by movement information. Hence it is possible that different tasks are dependent on different input modules, and that combination of the inputs to form a single representation is not useful.

OBJECT REPRESENTATION

No matter how efficient and rich the description produced in the stages described so far, the most fundamental and difficult step in visual recognition is the matching of this description to some pre-stored representation of an object. This is the very essence of recognition, allowing us to mobilize our existing knowledge and thus to make sense of the world. The processes involved in matching the viewer-centred representation provided by the $2\frac{1}{2}$D sketch to stored representations are so complex that computational theories can provide only very general constraints. However, two basic requirements on any general method of representing objects are, first, that it be flexible enough to capture a wide range (if not all) recognizable objects, and second, that it be easily accessible from the types of representation available from the image. Of course, these requirements work both ways – a good way to represent objects will almost certainly suggest an appropriate way to describe the image, while a good way to describe the image will constrain the plausible ways of representing objects.

The representation provided by the $2\frac{1}{2}$D sketch is viewer-centred, describing the scene from one particular viewpoint, whereas pre-stored representations must obviously be much more general, describing the basic 3D structure of an object in such a way that its appearance from *any* viewpoint can easily be obtained. One effective way to achieve this is to describe the object, or a significant component of it, in relation to some axis – perhaps an axis of symmetry, or along which the object is most elongated or, failing these, an external reference such as vertical. Marr and Nishihara (1978) developed this basic idea into a representational scheme based upon generalized cones. A generalized cone has three components – an axis of description, a description of the cross-section at right-angles to this axis, and a description of how this basic cross-section varies along the axis. Thus, for example, the shape of a milk bottle would be completely described by an axis running lengthways through its centre, a circular cross-section, and a simple mathematical function specifying how the radius of the circle varies along the axis from top to bottom. Allowing that complex objects can be broken down into simpler 3D components, one can imagine similar descriptions of basic tree-shapes, or human beings – indeed almost anything can be represented by this scheme, although it is obviously more appropriate for some objects than for others.

Accessing models from the $2\frac{1}{2}$D sketch

A primary aim in coding the parts of an object relative to an axis is to derive a representation that is robust to the effects of changing viewpoint. For example, let us suppose that a coffee pot is coded as having a semi-circular handle connecting along the main elongated axis of the pot, with a lip on the other side of the main axis. This description of the parts relative to the main axis remains the same as the pot is rotated during the action of pouring, even though the description of the pot on the retina changes with the angle of rotation. All that is needed is that the main axis can be coded as such across the different orientations.

Of course, many common objects contain multiple axes: while the main axis of a coffee pot may be the axis of elongation determined by its height, there are other major axes for each of the parts – e.g., axes of symmetry for the handle and for the lip. The coffee pot can serve as the "object" for the visual system, if the other axes are coded as parts relative to the main axis of the pot. However, it is also possible for the lip to serve as the "object", in which case the parts might be the curved outer lines of the lip which are coded relative to the main axis of symmetry down the centre. These different descriptions might be used on different occasions. The lip might be taken as the "object" if the task is to discriminate the type of lip on the particular pot; however, if the task is to discriminate the type of coffee pot, then the lip would be coded as a part relative to whole pot.

The above discussion suggests that it might be useful to encode objects hierarchically, with each "part" nested relative to the main axis of the next-most global whole. For instance, this would allow an observer to focus upon a part, or to re-orient attention from a part to a whole, according to the task at hand. Marr and Nishihara's (1978) representation scheme allows this to take place.

Marr and Nishihara also recognized that such representations should probably not be static. For many objects, the locations of parts change as the whole object moves. Too rigid a coding of the location of a part to the whole could lead to the object becoming unrecognizable when it moves. In fact, human vision copes extremely well with motion of parts of objects, and can even use relative motion of parts as an important cue in recognizing complex perceptual wholes. Thus, in a classic demonstration, Johansson (1973) had stooges walk with light-points attached to the main joints of their bodies. Observers could see only the light-points as the stooges moved but they nevertheless gained the instantaneous impression of human beings walking. This instantaneous impression could be gained only if the coding of parts to the whole were sensitive to the ways in which the parts are articulated during movement of the object. Marr and Nishihara suggested that the locations of the parts of objects were coded with some degree of freedom of movement.

Comments, criticisms, and extensions

Marr and Nishihara's scheme for high-level object representations itself depends on adequate procedures for finding appropriate axes and for segmenting whole objects into suitable parts. Marr and Nishihara suggested that such segmentation may involve finding points of high concavity (sharp bends) along the bounding contour of an object, and segmenting the object at those points. The parts may then be coded as the regions divided by each region of concavity. Subsequent workers (e.g., Hoffman & Richards, 1984) have developed the formal computational theory demonstrating mathematically why regions of concavity provide reliable segmentation cues, and have demonstrated empirically that such regions are used for parsing wholes into parts in human vision.

Other empirical research shows that objects can be identified most rapidly at particular levels of specificity. For instance, cats may be identified first as animals, then as cats and then as a particular breed of cat (e.g., Rosch, Mervis, Gray, Johnson, & Boyes-Bream, 1976). This meshes with the notion of a hierarchical representation, with more specific representations being generated lower in the representational hierarchy. Hierarchical representations may also be computationally useful in that they allow fast access to more general levels of representational knowledge, and thus general categorization to be made rapidly.

Biederman: recognition by components (RBC) theory

Later researchers have queried details of Marr's account of object representation and recognition. One noteworthy extension was suggested by Biederman

42

(1987). Biederman's account differs in two fundamental ways from that proposed by Marr. First, instead of generalized cones, Biederman suggests that objects are represented in terms of a limited set of specific "geons" (which can be thought of as specific instances of generalized cones). Second, geons are derived by combining "non-accidental properties" typically found in images, for example a straight line in an image will generally indicate a straight 3D edge, a symmetrical region in the image will generally indicate a symmetrical 3D surface. These 2D image properties are reliable in the sense that they almost always indicate a related 3D property of the world.

Geons are specified by describing both the cross-section and the axis of a part of an object in terms of simple dichotomies (e.g., straight *vs* curved, symmetrical *vs* asymmetrical): there is no need to describe the degree of curvature or the actual shape of any symmetry. This provides a vocabulary of 36 geons, and objects can be described as a set of geons and their relationships. Recognition thus becomes a matter of (1) segmenting the image into regions (as done by Marr & Nishihara, 1978), (2) describing the regions in terms of their properties (straight, symmetrical, and so forth) to obtain a suitable description, and then (3) matching this description to a pre-stored geon-based description of known objects. The important point here, however, is that the initial descriptions can be obtained directly from a 2D representation (say the full primal sketch) because the whole scheme is based upon non-accidental image properties: there is no need to derive a $2\frac{1}{2}$D sketch.

Biederman's scheme is computationally useful in a number of ways. First, since it uses non-accidental properties of edges to drive the recognition process, it is robust to random noise in images. Second, since the coding of geons depends on qualitative rather than metric differences in image primitives, recognition does not depend on accurate metric representation (though whether visually guided actions to objects depend on metric information is perhaps another matter). Third, qualitative differences between the geon types are relatively constant across a wide range of image variations. It follows that the same descriptions of an object can be derived across a wide range of viewpoints, doing away with the need to generate complex 3D model representations to ease memory constraints on recognition.

In a number of ways, then, Biederman's account amounts to a different computational theory from that proposed by Marr, based on the realization that some 2D properties of images provide reliable information about the 3D structure of the world. Relevant empirical research indicates that object recognition may operate directly from 2D image properties (Biederman & Ju, 1988), though the extent to which it does so may differ according to the nature of the object (e.g., surface information may become useful when objects have to be differentiated within classes of visually similar neighbours; Price & Humphreys, 1989). Both edge-based processes, of the type suggested by Biederman, and surface-based processes, such as those proposed by Marr, may play a role in human object recognition.

CONCLUSIONS

From the examples considered, it should be clear that the product of a computational theory is, in practice, a set of specific constraints. An analysis of the stimulus, for example, may reveal constraints on its structure which may be exploited by building general assumptions into the analytic processes. Such is the case in edge detection and stereopsis, where the relationship between the images and the world leads almost directly to suggestions about specific neural processes, and the computational theory provides the link between neurophysiological, psychophysical, and computer modelling data. In other cases, the constraints emerge mainly from an analysis of the task, rather than the stimulus. Here, as in the case of object representation, the constraints typically function at a higher level and, although they are usually too general to suggest specific neural implementations, they none the less usefully restrict the range of possible solutions.

The computational approach that we have discussed in most detail, that of David Marr, was unremittingly bottom-up in emphasis. It sought to maximize the processing of image data, making only general assumptions about the nature of the perceptual world, rather than using assumptions about specific objects. In part, this may have been a reaction against the earlier "blocks world" research, which tended towards solutions too particular to the stimulus domain to be generally applicable. However, attempts to implement the processing algorithms proposed by Marr have not yet led to clear practical successes, and researchers are beginning again to consider whether top-down, domain-specific knowledge might be utilized (though, in contrast to the "blocks world" research, this would now be based on a thorough analysis of real-world image properties). This trend has been encouraged by two of the recent developments we have mentioned. One is the development of connectionist models of visual processing. In many instances, connectionist models incorporate feedback from higher-level representations to early representations, which can serve to constrain the "hypotheses" suggested by early visual processing. Within the models, the role of top-down feedback becomes more important as bottom-up information becomes more degenerate (e.g., McClelland, 1987), consistent with much evidence for top-down effects in vision. The second development stems from the work of researchers such as Biederman, who has argued that stored knowledge about objects may be contacted directly from 2D information in the image, without the elaboration of $2\frac{1}{2}$D or 3D descriptions. Direct edge-based activation provides a route for the early mobilization of object knowledge, and such early mobilization is clearly important if top-down processing is to play a role in normal object recognition. Indeed, the coupling of fast edge-based

processes to Marr and Nishihara's scheme of hierarchical object representation may provide one way to generate rapid object categorization and
top-down feedback using categorical knowledge.

In sum, we may expect to see a continuing and substantial modification of
the specific framework proposed by Marr. Nevertheless, his general
approach, and in particular the argument for computational theories, is
likely to remain as one of the most important contributions of research in
artificial intelligence to psychological theory. Such theories are able to guide
empirical and theoretical research, even if the detailed models specified at any
one time later turn out to be wrong.

FURTHER READING

Bowden, M. A. (1987). *Artificial intelligence & natural man* (2nd edn). London:
Massachusetts Institute of Technology Press.

Fischler, M. A., & Firschein, O. (Eds) (1987). *Readings in computer vision: Issues,
problems, principles, and paradigms.* Los Altos, CA: Morgan Kaufmann.

Green, P., & Bruce, V. (1991). *Visual perception* (2nd edn). London: Lawrence
Erlbaum.

Marr, D. (1982). *Vision: A computational investigation into human representation
and processing of visual information.* San Francisco, CA: Freeman.

Watt, R. J. (1991). *Understanding vision.* London: Academic Press.

REFERENCES

Adelson, E. H., & Movshon, J. A. (1982). Phenomenal coherence of moving visual
patterns. *Nature, 300,* 523–525.

Biederman, I. (1987). Recognition-by-components: A theory of human image understanding. *Psychological Review, 94,* 115–147.

Biederman, I., & Ju, G. (1988). Surface versus edge-based determinants of visual
recognition. *Cognitive Psychology, 20,* 38–64.

Blake, A., & Marinos, C. (1990) Shape from texture: Estimation, isotropy and
moments. *Artificial Intelligence, 45,* 323–380.

Canny, J. F. (1986). A computational approach to edge detection. *IEEE Transactions
on Pattern Analysis and Machine Intelligence, 8,* 679–698.

Clocksin, W. H. (1980). Perception of surface slant and edge labels from optical flow:
A computational approach. *Perception, 9,* 253–269.

Clowes, M. B. (1971). On seeing things. *Artificial Intelligence, 21,* 79–116.

Draper, S. W. (1981). The use of gradient and dual space in line-drawing interpretation. *Artificial Intelligence, 17,* 461–508.

Enns, J., & Rensink, R. A. (1990). Influence of scene-based properties on visual
search. *Science, 247,* 721–723.

Gibson, J. J. (1979). *The ecological approach to visual perception.* Boston, MA:
Houghton Mifflin.

Gray, C. M., & Singer, W. (1989). Stimulus specific neuronal oscillations in
orientation columns of cat visual cortex. *Proceedings of the National Academy of
Science, 86,* 1698–1702.

Grossberg, S., & Mingolla, E. (1985). Natural dynamics of perceptual grouping: texture boundaries and emergent segmentations. *Perception and Psychophysics*, *38*, 141–161.

Guzman, A. (1968). Decomposition of a visual scene into three-dimensional bodies. *Proceedings of the American Federation of Information Processing Studies Fall Joint Conference*, *33*, 291–304.

Harris, M. G. (1986). The perception of moving stimuli: A model of spatiotemporal coding in human vision. *Vision Research*, *26*, 1281–1287.

Hawken, M. J., & Parker, A. J. (1987). Spatial properties of neurons in the monkey striate cortex. *Proceedings of the Royal Society of London* B, *231*, 251–288.

Heeger, D. J. (1987). Model for the extraction of image flow. *Journal of the Optical Society of America*, *4A*, 1455–1471.

Hochstein, S., & Spitzer, H. (1984). Zero-crossing detectors in monkey cortex? *Biological Cybernetics*, *51*, 195–199.

Hoffman, D. D., & Richards, W. A. (1984). Parts of recognition. *Cognition*, *18*, 65–96.

Horn, B. K. P. (1977) Understanding image intensities. *Artificial Intelligence*, *8*, 201–231.

Hubel, D. H., & Wiesel, T. N. (1962). Receptive fields, binocular interaction and functional architecture in the cat's visual cortex. *Journal of Physiology*, *160*, 106–154.

Hubel, D. H., & Wiesel, T. N. (1968). Receptive fields and functional architecture in the cat's visual cortex. *Journal of Physiology*, *195*, 215–243.

Huffman, D. A. (1971). Impossible objects as nonsense sentences. *Machine Intelligence*, *6*, 295–324.

Hummel, J. E., & Biederman, I. (1992). Dynamic binding in a neural network for shape recognition. *Psychological Review*, *99*, 480–517.

Johansson, G. (1973). Visual perception of biological motion and a model for its analysis. *Perception and Psychophysics*, *14*, 201–211.

Julesz, B. (1971). *Foundations of cyclopean perception*. Chicago, IL: University of Chicago Press.

Kanade, T. (1981). Recovery of the 3-D shape of an object from a single view. *Artificial Intelligence*, *17*, 409–460.

Koenderink, J. J. (1986). Optic flow. *Vision Research*, *26*, 161–180.

Longuet-Higgins, H. C., & Prazdny, K. (1980). The interpretation of a moving retinal image. *Proceedings of the Royal Society of London*, B, *208*, 385–397.

McClelland, J. L. (1987). The case for interactionism in language processing. In M. Coltheart (Ed.) *Attention and performance XII* (pp. 3–36). London: Lawrence Erlbaum.

Marr, D. (1982). *Vision: A computational investigation into human representation and processing of visual information*. San Francisco, CA: Freeman.

Marr, D., & Hildreth, E. (1980). Theory of edge detection. *Proceedings of the Royal Society of London*, B, *207*, 187–217.

Marr, D., & Nishihara, K. H. (1978). Representation and recognition of the spatial organisation of three-dimensional shapes. *Proceedings of the Royal Society of London*, B, *200*, 269–294.

Marr, D., & Poggio, T. (1976). Cooperative computation of stereo disparity. *Science*, *194*, 283–287.

Marr, D., & Poggio, T. (1979). A theory of human stereo vision. *Proceedings of the Royal Society of London*, B, *204*, 301–328.

Marr, D., & Ullman, S. (1981). Directional selectivity and its use in early visual processing. *Proceedings of the Royal Society of London*, B, *211*, 151–180.

Perkins, D. N. (1968). Cubic corners. *MIT Research Laboratory of Electronics Quarterly Progress Report, 89,* 207–214.

Peterhans, E., & von der Heydt, R. (1989). Mechanisms of contour perception in monkey visual cortex 2: Contours bridging gaps. *Journal of Neuroscience, 9,* 1749–1763.

Pollard, S. B., Mayhew, J. E. W., & Frisby, J. P. (1985). PMF: A stereo correspondence algorithm using a disparity gradient limit. *Perception, 14,* 449–470.

Price, C. J., & Humphreys, G. W. (1989). The effects of surface detail on object categorization and naming. *Quarterly Journal of Experimental Psychology, 41A,* 797–828.

Rieger, J. H., & Lawton, D. T. (1985). Processing differential image motion. *Journal of the Optical Society of America, 2A,* 354–360.

Robson J. G. (1980). Neural images: The physiological basis of spatial vision. In C. S. Harris (Ed.) *Visual coding and adaptability* (pp. 177–214). Hillsdale, NJ: Lawrence Erlbaum.

Rosch, E., Mervis, C. B., Gray, W. D., Johnson, D. M., & Boyes-Bream, P. (1976). Basic objects in natural categories. *Cognitive Psychology, 8,* 382–439.

Tootell, R. B., Silverman, M. S., & De Valois, R. L. (1981). Spatial frequency columns in striate visual cortex. *Science, 214,* 813–815.

Ullman, S. (1979). *The interpretation of visual motion.* Cambridge, MA: Massachusetts Institute of Technology Press.

Waltz, D. (1975). Understanding line drawings as scenes with shadows. In P. H. Winston (Ed.) *The psychology of computer vision* (pp. 19–91). New York: McGraw-Hill.

Watson, A. B., & Ahumada, A. J. (1989). A hexagonal orthogonal-oriented pyramid as a model of image representation in the visual cortex. *IEEE Transactions on Biomedical Engineering, 36,* 97–106.

Watt, R. J. (1991). *Understanding vision.* London: Academic Press.

Watt, R. J., & Morgan, M. J. (1985). A theory of the primitive spatial code in human vision. *Vision Research, 25,* 1661–1674.

Waxman, A. M., & Wohn, K. (1988). Image flow theory: A framework for 3-D inference from time-varying imagery. In C. Brown (Ed.) *Advances in computer vision* (vol. 1, pp. 165–224). Hillsdale, NJ: Lawrence Erlbaum.

Wertheimer, M. (1912). Experimentalle Studien über der Sehen von Bewegung. *Zeitschrift für Psychologie, 61,* 161–265. Translated in T. Shipley (Ed.) (1961) *Classics in psychology.* New York: Philosophical Library.

Wilson, H. R., & Bergen, J. R. (1979). A four mechanism model for threshold spatial vision. *Vision research, 19,* 19–32.

47

3

HEARING

Brian C. J. Moore
University of Cambridge, England

This chapter is mainly concerned with the perception of sound by normally hearing and hearing-impaired people. However, to reach an understanding of the mechanisms involved in auditory perception, it is helpful to have a basic understanding of the physical nature of sounds and of the physiology of the peripheral auditory system. Hence the chapter starts with a brief review of those topics.

THE PHYSICAL CHARACTERISTICS OF SOUNDS

Fourier analysis

Sound usually originates from the motion or vibration of an object. This motion is impressed upon the surrounding medium (usually air) as a pattern of changes in pressure. The pressure changes are transmitted through the medium and may be heard as sound. One of the simplest types of sound is the sinusoid. For a sinusoid, the pressure variation as a function of time, $P(t)$, is described by the equation

$$P(t) = A \sin(2\pi ft)$$

where t is time, A is the peak amplitude (maximum deviation from the mean atmospheric pressure), and f is the frequency of the sound in Hz (number of cycles per second). A sinusoid has a "pure" tone quality, like the sound produced by a tuning fork, and is also called a "pure tone" or "simple tone".

Although any sound can be described in terms of sound pressure as a function of time (often called the waveform of the sound), it is often more convenient, and more meaningful, to describe sound in a different way, based on a theorem by Fourier, who proved that any complex waveform (with certain restrictions) can be analysed, or broken down, into a series of sinusoids with specific frequencies and amplitudes. Such an analysis is called Fourier analysis, and each sinusoid is called a (Fourier) component of the complex sound. A plot of the magnitudes of the components as a function of frequency is referred to as the spectrum of the sound.

The simplest type of complex sound to which Fourier analysis can be applied is one which is periodic, repeating regularly as a function of time. Such a sound is composed of a number of sinusoids, each of which has a frequency that is an integral multiple of the frequency of a common (not necessarily present) fundamental component. The fundamental component has a frequency equal to the repetition rate of the complex waveform as a whole. The frequency components of the complex sound are known as harmonics and are numbered, the fundamental being given harmonic number 1. The nth harmonic has a frequency which is n times that of the fundamental.

One of the reasons for representing sounds in terms of their sinusoidal components is that people can, to a limited extent, perform a similar analysis. For example, two simultaneous sinusoids, whose frequencies are not too close, will usually be heard as two separate tones each with its own pitch rather than as a single complex sound.

The measurement of sound level

The instruments used to measure the magnitudes of sounds, such as micro-phones, normally respond to changes in air pressure. However, the auditory system can deal with a huge range of sound pressures. This makes it inconvenient to deal with sound pressures directly. Instead a logarithmic measure expressing the ratio of two pressures is used – the decibel. One pressure, P_0, is chosen as a reference and the other pressure, P_1, is expressed relative to this. The number of decibels (dB) corresponding to a given ratio of acoustic pressure is

number of dB $= 20 \log_{10}(P_1/P_0)$.

When the magnitude of a sound is specified in dB, it is customary to use the word "level" to refer to its magnitude. The reference pressure most commonly used is 2×10^{-5} Newtons per square metre (N/m^2). A sound level specified using this reference level is referred to as a sound pressure level (SPL). The reference sound level, 0 dB SPL, is a low sound level which was chosen to be close to the average human threshold for detecting a 1,000-Hz sinusoid. Normal conversation typically has a level of 65–70 dB SPL, while a rock band may produce potentially damaging levels as high as 120 dB SPL.

BASIC STRUCTURE AND FUNCTION OF THE AUDITORY SYSTEM

The outer and middle ear

Figure 1 shows the structure of the peripheral part of the human auditory system. The outer ear is composed of the pinna (the part we actually see) and the auditory canal or meatus. Sound travels down the meatus and causes the eardrum, or tympanic membrane, to vibrate. These vibrations are transmitted through the middle ear by three small bones, the ossicles, to a membrane-covered opening (the oval window) in the bony wall of the spiral-shaped structure of the inner ear – the cochlea. Damage to the middle ear, or obstruction of the ear canal, leads to a partial hearing loss known as conductive deafness. Its effects are similar to a simple attenuation of the sound, and it can often be treated medically.

The inner ear and the basilar membrane

The cochlea is divided along its length by the basilar membrane, which moves in response to sound. The response of the basilar membrane to sinusoidal stimulation takes the form of a travelling wave which moves along the membrane, with an amplitude that increases at first and then decreases rather abruptly. The basic form of the wave is illustrated in Figure 2, which shows

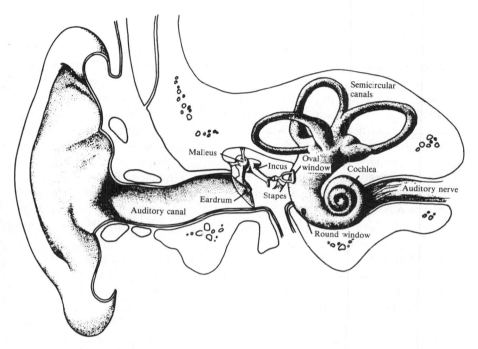

Figure 1 Illustration of the structure of the peripheral auditory system showing the outer, middle and inner ear
Source: Lindsay and Norman, 1972, by permission of the authors

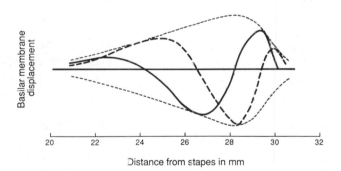

Figure 2 The instantaneous displacement of the basilar membrane at two successive instants in time, derived from a cochlear model. The pattern moves from left to right, building up gradually with distance, and decaying rapidly beyond the point of maximal displacement. The dotted line represents the envelope traced out by the amplitude peaks in the waveform
Source: Redrawn from von Békésy, 1947

51

the instantaneous displacement of the basilar membrane (derived from a cochlear model, described by von Békésy, 1947) for two successive instants in time, in response to a 200-Hz sinusoid. This figure also shows the line joining the amplitude peaks, which is called the envelope. The envelope shows a peak at a particular position on the basilar membrane.

The position of the peak in the pattern of vibration differs according to the frequency of stimulation. High-frequency sounds (around 15,000 Hz) produce a peak near the oval window, while low-frequency sounds (around 50 Hz) produce a peak towards the other end (the apex). Intermediate frequencies produce peaks at intermediate places. Thus, each point on the basilar membrane is "tuned" to a particular frequency. When a sound is composed of several sinusoids with different frequencies, each sinusoid produces a peak at its own characteristic place on the basilar membrane. In effect, the cochlea behaves like a Fourier analyser, although with a less than perfect frequency-analysing power.

Measurements of basilar membrane vibration have shown that the basilar membrane is much more sharply tuned than originally found by von Békésy (1960). The sharpness of tuning of the basilar membrane depends critically on physiological condition; the better the condition, the sharper is the tuning (Khanna & Leonard, 1982; Robles, Ruggero, & Rich, 1986). In a normal, healthy ear, each point on the basilar membrane is sharply tuned, responding with high sensitivity to a limited range of frequencies, and requiring higher and higher sound intensities to produce a response as the frequency is made higher or lower. The sharp tuning and high sensitivity probably reflect an active process; that is, they do not result simply from the mechanical properties of the basilar membrane and surrounding fluid, but depend on biological structures actively influencing the mechanics (for reviews, see Pickles, 1986, 1988; Yates, 1986). Damage to the cochlea can weaken or destroy the active process, leading to a type of hearing loss known as cochlear hearing loss. This results not only in a loss of sensitivity to weak sounds (an elevation of the absolute threshold), but also in changes in the way that supra-threshold sounds are perceived. Cochlear hearing loss usually cannot be helped by medical treatment.

Between the basilar membrane and the tectorial membrane are hair cells, which form part of a structure called the organ of Corti (see Figure 3). The hair cells are divided into two groups by an arch known as the tunnel of Corti. Those on the side of the arch closest to the outside of the cochlea are known as outer hair cells, and are arranged in three rows in the cat and up to five rows in humans. The hair cells on the other side of the arch form a single row, and are known as inner hair cells. There are about 25,000 outer hair cells, while there are about 3,500 inner hair cells. The tectorial membrane, which has a gelatinous structure, lies above the hairs. When the basilar membrane moves up and down, a shearing motion is created between the basilar membrane and the tectorial membrane. As a result the hairs at the

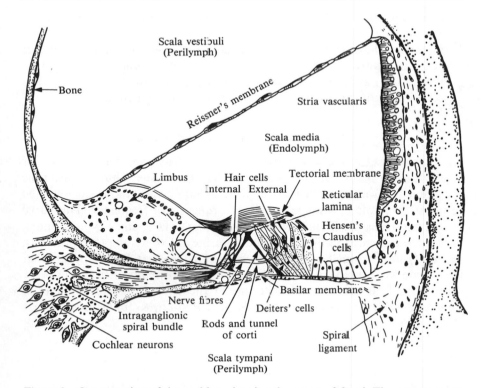

Figure 3 Cross-section of the cochlea, showing the organ of Corti. The receptors are the hair cells lying on either side of the tunnel of Corti
Source: Redrawn from Davis, 1962

tops of the hair cells are displaced. It is thought that this leads to excitation of the inner hair cells, which leads in turn to the generation of action potentials in the neurons of the auditory nerve. Thus the inner hair cells act to transduce mechanical movements into neural activity.

The main role of the outer hair cells may be actively to influence the mechanics of the cochlea, so as to produce high sensitivity and sharp tuning. There is even evidence that the outer hair cells have a motor function, changing their length and shape in response to electrical stimulation (for a review see Pickles, 1988). Cochlear hearing loss is often associated with damage to the outer hair cells.

NEURAL RESPONSES IN THE AUDITORY NERVE

Information in the auditory nerve is carried in three main ways:

1 In terms of the rate of firing (action potentials per second) within

individual neurons. Generally, increases in sound level result in increases in firing rate.

2 In terms of the distribution of activity across neurons. This reflects the fact that each neuron is tuned to a particular frequency range.

3 In terms of the detailed time pattern of firing of individual neurons. The second and third of these will be described in more detail.

Tuning curves in the auditory nerve

Each neuron in the auditory nerve derives its activity from one or more hair cells lying at a particular place on the basilar membrane. Thus, the neurons are "tuned". This is often illustrated by a tuning curve, which shows the response threshold of a single neuron as a function of frequency. This curve is also known as the frequency-threshold curve (FTC). Some typical tuning curves are presented in Figure 4. The frequency at which the threshold of a neuron is lowest is called the characteristic frequency (CF). It appears that the sharpness of tuning of the basilar membrane is essentially the same as the sharpness of tuning of single neurons in the auditory nerve (Khanna & Leonard, 1982; Robles et al., 1986; Sellick, Patuzzi, & Johnstone, 1982).

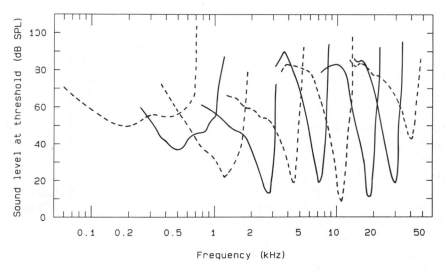

Figure 4 A sample of tuning curves (also called frequency-threshold curves) obtained from single neurons in the auditory nerve of anaesthetized cats. Each curve shows results for one neuron. The sound level required for threshold is plotted as a function of the stimulus frequency (logarithmic scale)
Source: Redrawn from Palmer, 1987

Phase locking

Nerve firings tend to be phase locked or synchronized to the time pattern of the stimulating waveform. A given neuron does not necessarily fire on every cycle of the stimulus but, when firings do occur, they occur at roughly the same phase of the waveform each time (e.g., close to a peak). Thus the time intervals between firings are (approximately) integral multiples of the period of the stimulating waveform. For example, a 500-Hz sinusoid has a period of 2 milliseconds (2 ms), and the intervals between nerve firings in response to it are grouped around 2 ms, 4 ms, 6 ms, and 8 ms. Phase locking becomes less precise at high frequencies, and in most mammals cannot be measured for frequencies above about 5 kHz.

THE ACTION OF THE EAR AS A FREQUENCY ANALYSER

A major characteristic of the auditory system is that it acts as a limited-resolution frequency analyser; complex sounds are broken down into their sinusoidal frequency components. The initial basis of this frequency analysis almost certainly depends upon the tuning which is observed on the basilar membrane. Largely as a consequence of this analysis, we are able to hear one sound in the presence of another sound with a different frequency. This ability is known as frequency selectivity or frequency resolution.

Measurement of the ear's frequency selectivity

Important sounds are sometimes rendered inaudible by other sounds, a process known as "masking". Masking may be considered as a failure of frequency selectivity, and it can be used as a tool to measure the frequency selectivity of the ear. One conception of masking, which has had both theoretical and practical success, assumes that the auditory system contains a bank of overlapping band-pass filters, with adjacent, ordered, centre frequencies (Fletcher, 1940; Patterson & Moore, 1986). The filters are called the "auditory filters". In the simple case of a sinusoidal signal presented in a background noise, it is assumed that the observer detects the signal using the filter whose output has the highest signal-to-masker ratio. The signal is detected if that ratio exceeds a certain value. In most practical situations, the filter involved has a centre frequency close to that of the signal.

A good deal of work has been directed towards determining the characteristics of the auditory filters; the most important characteristic for a given filter is the relative response to different frequencies, sometimes referred to as the "shape" of the filter. One method uses a psychophysical analogue of the method used by neurophysiologists to determine a neural tuning curve. The resulting curves are often called psychophysical tuning curves (PTCs). The signal used is a sinusoid which is usually presented at a very low level, say 10 dB above the absolute threshold. It is assumed that this will excite only a small number of nerve fibres with characteristic frequencies (CFs) close to that of the signal. Thus, to a first approximation, only one auditory filter will be involved in detecting the signal. The masker is either a sinusoid or a noise containing a narrow range of frequencies.

To determine a PTC the signal is fixed in frequency and level, and the level of the masker required to mask the signal is determined, for various centre frequencies of the masker. If it is assumed that the signal will be masked when the masker produces a fixed amount of activity in the neurons that would otherwise respond to the signal, then the curve mapped out in this way is analogous to the neural tuning curve. Some examples are given in Figure 5. Returning to the concept of the auditory filter, we can think of the PTC as representing the masker level required to produce a fixed output from the filter centred at the signal frequency. Thus the filter "shape" can be obtained simply by turning the tuning curve upside-down.

An alternative method of determining the auditory filter shape has been described by Patterson (1976). The method is illustrated in Figure 6. The signal is fixed in frequency, and the masker is a noise with a bandstop or notch centred at the signal frequency. The deviation of each edge of the notch from the signal frequency is denoted by Δf. The threshold of the signal is

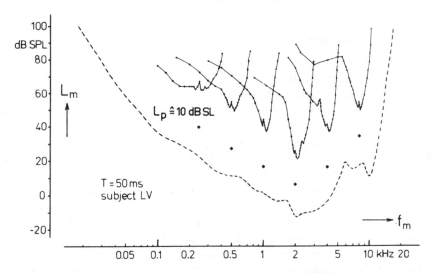

Figure 5 Psychophysical tuning curves (PTCs) determined in simultaneous masking using sinusoidal signals 10 dB above absolute threshold (called 10 dB SL). For each curve the solid diamond below it indicates the frequency and level of the signal. The masker was a sinusoid which had a fixed starting phase relationship to the 50-ms signal. The masker level required for threshold is plotted as a function of masker frequency. The dashed line shows the absolute threshold for the signal

Source: From Vogten, 1974, by permission of the author

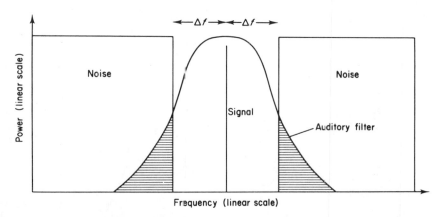

Figure 6 Schematic illustration of the method used by Patterson (1976) to determine auditory filter shape. The threshold of the sinusoidal signal is measured as a function of the width of a spectral notch in the noise masker. The amount of noise passing through the auditory filter centred at the signal frequency is proportional to the shaded areas

Source: Moore, 1989

determined as a function of notch width. Usually the notch is symmetrically placed around the signal frequency and the analysis assumes that the auditory filter is symmetric on a linear frequency scale. This assumption seems reasonable at moderate sound levels (Patterson & Moore, 1986).

As the width of the notch is increased, less and less noise passes through the auditory filter; thus, the threshold of the signal drops, that is, improves. The amount of noise passing through the auditory filter is proportional to the area under the filter in the frequency range covered by the noise. This is shown as the shaded areas in Figure 6. Given the assumption that threshold corresponds to a constant signal-to-masker ratio at the output of the auditory filter, the change in threshold with notch width indicates how the area under the filter varies with Δf. From this, it is possible to derive the shape of the filter itself. The method can also be extended to the case where the filter is not assumed to be symmetric, provided certain assumptions are made about the general form of the filter (Patterson & Moore, 1986).

A typical auditory filter shape obtained using Patterson's method is shown in Figure 7, for a centre frequency of 1 kHz. Notice that the filter is symmetrical on the linear frequency scale used; this is only the case at moderate sound levels. The sharpness of a filter is often described by its equivalent rectangular bandwidth (ERB). This is defined as the frequency range covered by a rectangular filter with the same peak value and which passes the same total power of white noise (a sound containing equal energy at all frequencies). The ERB of the auditory filter increases with increasing centre frequency. However, when expressed as a proportion of centre frequency the band-

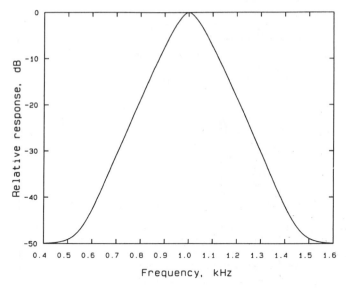

Figure 7 A typical auditory filter shape derived using Patterson's notched-noise method

width tends to be narrowest at middle to high frequencies. Over the range 100 to 8,000 Hz, and at moderate sound levels, the ERB (in Hz), is well approximated by

ERB = 24.7(4.37F + 1)

where F is frequency in kHz (Glasberg & Moore, 1990).

Frequency selectivity in the hearing impaired

There is now considerable evidence that in people with hearing impairments of cochlear origin there is a loss of frequency selectivity. This type of hearing loss is quite common, especially in elderly people. In general, higher absolute thresholds tend to be associated with broader auditory filters. Figure 8 shows a comparison of auditory filter shapes obtained separately from each ear of six subjects, each with a cochlear hearing loss in one ear only (data from Glasberg & Moore, 1986). The upper panels show filter shapes for the normal ears and the lower panels show filter shapes for the impaired ears, which had threshold elevations at the test frequency (1 kHz) ranging from about 40 to 60 dB. Losses were relatively flat as a function of frequency. A notched-noise masker was used, as described earlier, and the same noise level was used for testing all ears. It is clear that the auditory filters are considerably broader in the impaired ears. The most obvious feature is that the lower skirts of the filters are consistently and considerably less sharp than normal in the impaired ears.

A consequence of reduced frequency selectivity is a greater susceptibility to masking by interfering sounds. This may partly account for the fact that people with cochlear hearing loss often complain of difficulty in understanding speech in noise.

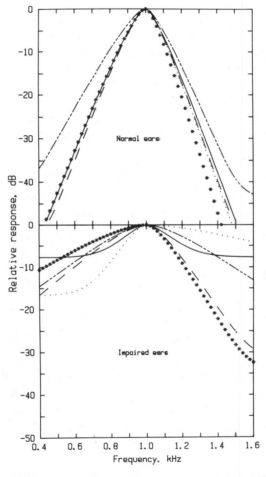

Figure 8 Auditory filter shapes for the normal ears (top) and the impaired ears (bottom) of six subjects with unilateral cochlear impairments. The impaired ear of subject DJ had too little frequency selectivity for a filter shape to be determined
Source: Glasberg and Moore, 1986

THE PERCEPTION OF LOUDNESS

Equal-loudness contours

In describing the perception of sound it is useful to have some kind of scale which allows one to compare the loudness of different sounds. A first step towards this is to construct equal-loudness contours for sinusoids of different frequencies. Say, for example, we take a standard tone of 1 kHz, at a level of 40 dB SPL, and ask the listener to adjust the level of a second tone (say, 2 kHz) so that it sounds equally loud. If we repeat this for many different frequencies of the second tone, then the sound level required, plotted as a function of frequency, maps out an equal-loudness contour. The level of the 1-kHz standard sound defines the loudness level, in phons. If we repeat this procedure, for different levels of the 1-kHz standard tone, then we will map out a family of equal loudness contours. Such a family is shown in Figure 9. Note that the contours resemble the absolute threshold curve (lowest curve in the figure) at low levels, but tend to become flatter at high levels.

The role of frequency selectivity in determining loudness

It has been known for many years that if the total intensity of a complex sound is fixed, its loudness depends on the frequency range over which the

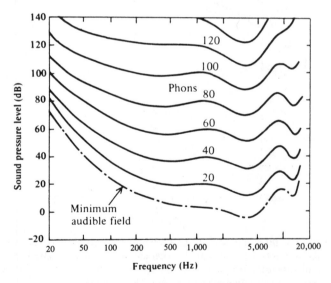

Figure 9 Equal-loudness contours for various loudness levels, as indicated on each curve. The dashed-dotted curve shows the absolute threshold (minimum audible field)
Source: Moore, 1989. Original data from Robinson and Dadson, 1956

sound extends. The basic mechanism underlying this seems to be the same auditory filter as is revealed in masking experiments. Consider as an example a noise whose total intensity is held constant while the bandwidth is varied. The loudness of the noise can be estimated indirectly by asking the listener to adjust the intensity of a second sound, with a fixed bandwidth, so that it sounds equally loud. The two sounds are presented successively. When the bandwidth of the noise is less than a certain value, the loudness is roughly independent of bandwidth. However, as the bandwidth is increased beyond a certain point, the loudness starts to increase. This is illustrated in Figure 10, for several different overall levels of the noise. The bandwidth at which loudness starts to increase is known as the critical bandwidth for loudness summation. Its value is approximately the same as the ERB of the auditory filter. A model which explains this effect is described by Moore and Glasberg (1986).

Loudness perception and recruitment in impaired ears

Cochlear hearing loss is usually associated with an abnormality of loudness perception known as loudness recruitment. Although the absolute threshold

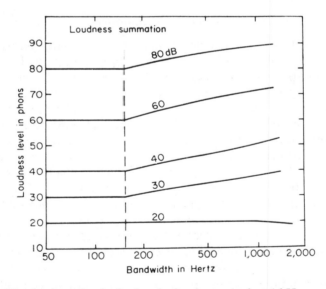

Figure 10 The loudness level of a band of noise centred at 1 kHz, measured as a function of the width of the band. For each of the curves the overall level was held constant, and is indicated in the figure. The dashed line shows that the bandwidth at which loudness begins to increase is the same at all levels tested (except that no increase occurs at the lowest level)

Source: Redrawn from Feldtkeller and Zwicker, 1956

may be elevated, the rate of growth of loudness with intensity is more rapid than normal, so that at high intensities a sound appears as loud in an impaired ear as it would in a normal ear. The effect is most easily demonstrated when only one ear of a person is affected, since then loudness matches can be made between the two ears, but it can be detected in other ways. The presence of recruitment can limit the usefulness of conventional hearing aids, since if the gain of the aid is set so as to make sounds of low intensity clearly audible, sounds of high intensity will be uncomfortably loud. Hearing aids incorporating automatic gain control (AGC), especially multi-band AGC, can be useful in alleviating this effect (Laurence, Moore, & Glasberg, 1983; Moore, 1987).

Loudness recruitment can probably be explained in terms of responses on the basilar membrane. In normal ears the active mechanism amplifies the response to weak sounds, but has progressively less effect at high sound levels. In impaired ears, this mechanism is damaged or inoperative. Thus weak sounds may not be detected, but the response to strong sounds is almost normal (Moore, 1989; Yates, 1990).

THE PERCEPTION OF PITCH

The pitch of sinusoids

Pitch is defined as that attribute of auditory sensation in terms of which sounds may be ordered on a musical scale, that is, that attribute in which variations constitute melody. For sinusoids (pure tones) the pitch is largely determined by the frequency; the higher the frequency the higher the pitch. One of the classic debates in hearing theory is concerned with the mechanisms underlying the perception of pitch. One theory, called the place theory, suggests that pitch is related to the position of maximum vibration on the basilar membrane, which is coded in terms of the relative activity of neurons with different CFs. Shifts in frequency will be detected as changes in the amount of activity at the place where the activity changes most. The alternative theory, the temporal theory, suggests that pitch is determined by the time-pattern of neural spikes (phase locking).

One major fact that these theories have to account for is our remarkably fine acuity in detecting frequency changes. This ability is called frequency discrimination, and is not to be confused with frequency selectivity. For two tones of 500 ms duration presented successively, a difference of about 3 Hz (or less in trained subjects) can be detected at a centre frequency of 1 kHz. It has been suggested that tuning curves (or auditory filters) are not sufficiently sharp to account for this fine acuity in terms of the place theory (Moore & Glasberg, 1986). A further difficulty for the place theory is that frequency discrimination worsens abruptly above 4–5 kHz (Moore, 1973). Neither neural measures of frequency selectivity (such as tuning curves) nor psychophysical measures of frequency selectivity (such as PTCs or auditory filter shapes) show any abrupt change there.

These facts can be explained by assuming that temporal mechanisms are dominant at frequencies below 4–5 kHz. Changes in frequency discrimination with centre frequency (and with tone duration) can be predicted from the information available in inter-spike intervals (Goldstein & Srulovicz, 1977). The worsening performance at 4–5 kHz corresponds well with the frequency at which the temporal information ceases to be available. Studies of our perception of musical intervals also indicate a change in mechanism around 4–5 kHz. Below this, a sequence of pure tones with appropriate frequencies conveys a clear sense of melody. Above this, the sense of musical interval and of melody is lost, although the changes in frequency may still be heard.

The evidence, then, supports the idea that, for pure tones, pitch perception and discrimination are determined primarily by temporal information for frequencies below 4–5 kHz, and by place information for frequencies above this. The important frequencies for the perception of music and speech lie in the frequency range where temporal information is available.

The pitch perception of complex tones

In general, any complex sound that is periodic has a pitch, provided that the waveform repetition rate lies in the range 20–16,000 Hz. If a listener is asked to adjust the frequency of a sinusoid so that its pitch matches that of a complex tone, the frequency is usually set close to the fundamental frequency of the complex. In other words, the pitch of the complex tone is the same as the pitch of its fundamental sinusoidal component. Remarkably, however, the fundamental component does not have to be present for this pitch to be heard; removing the fundamental component from a complex sound does not generally change its pitch, although the tone quality may be slightly altered. This is called the "phenomenon of the missing fundamental". It seems that the low pitch of a complex tone is somehow derived from its higher harmonics.

Most modern theories of pitch perception assume a two-stage process. In the first stage, the stimulus is passed through an array of filters (the auditory filters). These resolve (separate) the lower harmonics, but usually do not resolve the higher harmonics. In the second stage, the pitch is derived by a central processor from the pattern of the output of the auditory filters. The central processor may make use of the distribution of activity across auditory filters, the time patterns at the outputs of the filters, or both of these (Goldstein, 1973; Moore, 1989; Moore & Glasberg, 1986; Terhardt, 1974). In essence, the pitch corresponding to the missing fundamental appears to be derived by a kind of pattern recognition process from information conveyed by harmonics above the fundamental.

63

THE PERCEPTION OF TIMBRE

Timbre may be defined as the characteristic quality of sound that distinguishes one voice or musical instrument from another (when their pitches and loudnesses are the same). Timbre depends on several different physical properties of sound, including

1 Whether the sound is periodic, having a tonal quality for repetition rates from about 20 to 16,000 Hz, or irregular and having a noise-like quality.
2 Whether the sound is continuous or interrupted. For sounds that have short durations the exact way in which the sound is turned on and off can play an important role. For example, in the case of sounds produced by stringed instruments, a rapid onset (a fast rise time) is usually perceived as a struck or plucked string, whereas a gradual onset is heard as a bowed string.
3 The distribution of energy over frequency, and changes in the distribution with time. This is the correlate of timbre that has been studied most widely. Sounds containing predominantly high frequencies have a "sharp" timbre, whereas those containing mainly low frequencies sound "dull" or "mellow". This is another example of the action of the ear as a frequency analyser. The components in a complex sound will be partially separated by the auditory filters, and the distribution of activity at the output of the filters, as a function of filter centre frequency, determines timbre.

THE TEMPORAL RESOLUTION OF THE EAR

The auditory system is particularly well adapted to detecting changes in sounds as a function of time. The limits of this ability reflect the temporal resolution of the ear. One measure of this requires the subject to detect a brief gap in a relatively long duration sound. Many gap-detection experiments have used white noise as a stimulus; this noise contains equal energy at all frequencies. The results generally agree quite well, the threshold value being 2 to 3 ms (Penner, 1977; Plomp, 1964). More recently, gap thresholds have been measured for bandpass noises, to determine whether gap threshold varies with centre frequency. Unfortunately, when a noise band is abruptly switched off and on, to produce the gap, energy is spread to frequencies outside the nominal bandwidth of the noise. In order to prevent the detection of this "spectral splatter", which could give rise to artificially low thresholds, the noise bands have been presented in a continuous noise designed to mask the splatter (Fitzgibbons & Wightman, 1982; Shailer & Moore, 1983). Some results from Shailer and Moore (1983) are plotted in Figure 11.

The value of the gap threshold increases monotonically with decreasing centre frequency. At high frequencies the gap threshold is similar to that found for white noise, suggesting that subjects make use primarily of high

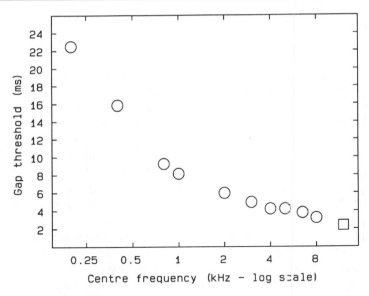

Figure 11 Thresholds for the detection of a temporal gap in a bandpass noise
stimulus, as a function of the centre frequency cf the noise
Source: Data from Shailer and Moore, 1983

frequencies when detecting gaps in white noise. The increase in gap threshold
at low frequencies may be connected with temporal fluctuations in the noise
bands. The auditory filters have narrower bandwidths at low frequencies,
and so each filter passes only a small range of frequencies; at low frequencies
the output is a narrow band of noise. A narrow band of noise resembles a
sinusoid that is fluctuating in amplitude from moment to moment. The
narrower the bandwidth, the slower are the fluctuations. Slow fluctuations in
the noise, especially "dips" in the envelope, may be confused with the gap
that is to be detected. Thus, the increase in gap threshold at low frequencies
may be explained by the decrease in auditory filter bandwidth, and the
resulting slow fluctuations at the output of the auditory filter.

Another way of measuring temporal resolution is to determine the
threshold for detecting amplitude modulation (changes in amplitude over
time) as a function of modulation rate; the resulting function is known as the
temporal modulation transfer function (TMTF). When the modulated
stimulus is white noise, modulation thresholds are small (i.e., sensitivity is
high) for modulation rates up to about 50 Hz, and thresholds increase
progressively beyond that (Viemeister, 1979). Modulation is not detectable at
all for rates above about 500–1,000 Hz.

THE LOCALIZATION OF SOUNDS

Binaural cues

It has long been recognized that slight differences in the sounds reaching the two ears can be used as cues in sound localization. The two major cues are differences in the time of arrival at the two ears and differences in intensity at the two ears. For example, a sound coming from the left will arrive first at the left ear and be more intense in the left ear. For steady sinusoidal stimulation, differences in time of arrival can be detected and used to judge location only at frequencies below about 1,500 Hz. At low frequencies, very small changes in relative time of arrival at the two ears can be detected, of about 10–20 μs, which is equivalent to a movement of the sound source of 1–2° laterally.

Intensity differences between the two ears are primarily useful at high frequencies. This is because low frequencies bend or diffract around the head, so that there is little difference in intensity at the two ears whatever the location of the sound source. At high frequencies the head casts more of an acoustic "shadow", and above 2–3 kHz the intensity differences are sufficient to provide useful cues. For complex sounds, containing a range of frequencies, the difference in spectral patterning at the two ears may also be important.

The idea that sound localization is based on interaural time differences at low frequencies and interaural intensity differences at high frequencies has been called the "duplex theory" of sound localization, and it dates back to Lord Rayleigh (1907). However, it has been realized that it is not quite correct (Hafter, 1984). Complex sounds containing only high frequencies (above 1,500 Hz) can be localized on the basis of interaural time delays, provided that they have an appropriate temporal structure. For example, a single click can be localized in this way no matter what its frequency content. Periodic sounds containing only high-frequency harmonics can also be localized on the basis of interaural time differences, provided that the envelope repetition rate is below about 600 Hz (Neutzel & Hafter, 1981). Since many of the complex sounds we encounter in everyday life have envelope repetition rates below 600 Hz, interaural time differences will be used for localization in most listening situations.

The role of the pinna

Binaural cues are not sufficient to account for all of our localization abilities. For example, a simple difference in time or intensity will not define whether a sound is coming from in front or behind, or above or below, but people can clearly make such judgements. It has been shown that the pinnae play an important role in sound localization (Batteau, 1967). They do so because the spectra of sounds entering the ear are modified by the pinnae in a way which depends upon the direction of the sound source. This direction-dependent filtering provides cues for sound source location. The cues occur mainly at high frequencies, above about 6 kHz. The pinnae are important not only for localization, but also for judging whether a sound comes from within the head or from the outside world. A sound is judged as coming from outside only if the spectral transformations characteristic of the pinnae are imposed on the sound. Thus sounds heard through headphones are normally judged as being inside the head; the pinnae do not have their normal effect on the sound when headphones are worn. However, sounds delivered by headphones can be made to appear to come from outside the head if the signals delivered to the headphones are prerecorded on a dummy head or synthetically processed (filtered) so as to mimic the normal action of the pinnae. Such processing can also create the impression of a sound coming from any desired direction in space.

The precedence effect

In everyday conditions, the sound from a given source reaches the ears by many different paths. Some of it arrives via a direct path, but a great deal may only reach the ears after reflections from one or more surfaces. However, people are not normally aware of these reflections or echoes, and they do not appear to impair the ability to localize sound sources. The reason for this seems to lie in a phenomenon known as the precedence effect (Wallach, Newman, & Rosenzweig, 1949). When several similar sounds reach our ears in close succession (i.e., the direct sound and its echoes) the sounds are perceptually fused into a single sound, and the location of the total sound is primarily determined by the location of the first (direct) sound. Thus the echoes have little influence on the perception of direction, although they may influence the timbre and loudness of the sound.

Sound localization in the hearing impaired

Most hearing losses result in some degradation in sound localization (Durlach, Thompson, & Colburn, 1981). However, there may be considerable individual differences even in people with similar amounts of hearing loss. In general, tumours in the auditory nerve, or damage higher up in the auditory pathways, lead to greater localization problems than cochlear losses. Most hearing-impaired people show a reduced ability to use interaural time and intensity differences. In addition, people with high-frequency hearing losses are generally unable to make use of the directional information provided by the pinnae. Hearing aid users also suffer in this respect, since, even if the microphone is appropriately placed within the pinna, the response of most aids is limited to frequencies below 6 kHz.

FURTHER READING

Bregman, A. S. (1990). *Auditory scene analysis: The perceptual organisation of sound*. Cambridge, MA: Bradford.

Moore, B. C. J. (1986). *Frequency selectivity in hearing*. London: Academic Press.

Moore, B. C. J. (1989). *An introduction to the psychology of hearing* (3rd edn). London: Academic Press.

Pickles, J. O. (1988). *An introduction to the physiology of hearing* (2nd edn). London: Academic Press.

REFERENCES

Batteau, D. W. (1967). The role of the Pinna in human localization. *Proceedings of the Royal Society*, B, *168*, 158–180.

Davis, H. (1962). Advances in the neurophysiology and neuroanatomy of the cochlea. *Journal of the Acoustical Society of America*, *34*, 1377–1385.

Durlach, N. I., Thompson, C. L., & Colburn, H. S. (1981). Binaural interaction in impaired listeners. *Audiology*, *20*, 181–211.

Feldtkeller, R., & Zwicker, E. (1956). *Das Ohr als Nachrichtenempfänger*. Stuttgart: S. Hirzel.

Fitzgibbons, P. J., & Wightman, F. L. (1982). Gap detection in normal and hearing-impaired listeners. *Journal of the Acoustical Society of America*, *72*, 761–765.

Fletcher, H. (1940). Auditory patterns. *Reviews of Modern Physics*, *12*, 47–65.

Glasberg, B. R., & Moore, B. C. J. (1986). Auditory filter shapes in subjects with unilateral and bilateral cochlear impairments. *Journal of the Acoustical Society of America*, *79*, 1020–1033.

Glasberg, B. R., & Moore, B. C. J. (1990). Derivation of auditory filter shapes from notched-noise data. *Hearing Research*, *47*, 103–138.

Goldstein, J. L. (1973). An optimum processor theory for the central formation of the pitch of complex tones. *Journal of the Acoustical Society of America*, *54*, 1496–1516.

Goldstein, J. L., & Srulovicz, P. (1977). Auditory-nerve spike intervals as an adequate basis for aural frequency measurement. In E. F. Evans & J. P. Wilson (Ed.) *Psychophysics and physiology of hearing* (pp. 337–346). London: Academic Press.

Hafter, E. R. (1984). Spatial hearing and the duplex theory: How viable? In G. M. Edelman, W. E. Gall, & W. M. Cowan (Eds) *Dynamic aspects of neocortical function* (pp. 425–448). New York: Wiley.

Khanna, S. M., & Leonard, D. G. B. (1982). Basilar membrane tuning in the cat cochlea. *Science*, *215*, 305–306.

Laurence, R. F., Moore, B. C. J., & Glasberg, B. R. (1983). A comparison of behind-the-ear high-fidelity linear aids and two-channel compression hearing aids in the laboratory and in everyday life. *British Journal of Audiology*, *17*, 31–48.

Lindsay, P. H., & Norman, D. A. (1972). *Human information processing*. New York and London: Academic Press.

Moore, B. C. J. (1973). Frequency difference limens for short-duration tones. *Journal of the Acoustical Society of America*, *54*, 610–619.

Moore, B. C. J. (1987). Design and evaluation of a two-channel compression hearing aid. *Journal of Rehabilitation Research and Development*, *24*, 181–192.

Moore, B. C. J. (1989). *An introduction to the psychology of hearing* (3rd edn). London: Academic Press.

Moore, B. C. J., & Glasberg, B. R. (1986). The role of frequency selectivity in the perception of loudness, pitch and time. In B. C. J. Moore (Ed.) *Frequency selectivity in hearing* (pp. 251–308). London: Academic Press.

Neutzel, J. M., & Hafter, E. R. (1981). Lateralization of complex waveforms: Spectral effects. *Journal of the Acoustical Society of America, 69,* 1112–1118.

Palmer, A. R. (1987). Physiology of the cochlear nerve and cochlear nucleus. In M. P. Haggard & E. F. Evans (Eds) *Hearing* (pp. 838–855). Edinburgh: Churchill Livingstone.

Patterson, R. D. (1976). Auditory filter shapes derived with noise stimuli. *Journal of the Acoustical Society of America, 59,* 640–654.

Patterson, R. D., & Moore, B. C. J. (1986). Auditory filters and excitation patterns as representations of frequency resolution. In B. C. J. Moore (Ed.) *Frequency selectivity in hearing* (pp. 123–177). London: Academic Press.

Penner, M. J. (1977). Detection of temporal gaps in noise as a measure of the decay of auditory sensation. *Journal of the Acoustical Society of America, 61,* 552–557.

Pickles, J. O. (1986). The neurophysiological basis of frequency selectivity. In B. C. J. Moore (Ed.) *Frequency selectivity in hearing* (pp. 51–121). London: Academic Press.

Pickles, J. O. (1988). *An introduction to the physiology of hearing* (2nd edn). London: Academic Press.

Plomp, R. (1964). The rate of decay of auditory sensation. *Journal of the Acoustical Society of America, 36,* 277–282.

Rayleigh, Lord (1907). On our perception of sound direction. *Philosophical Magazine, 13,* 214–232.

Robinson, D. W., & Dadson, R. S. (1956). A re-determination of the equal-loudness relations for pure tones. *British Journal of Applied Physics, 7,* 166–181.

Robles, L., Ruggero, M. A., & Rich, N. C. (1986). Basilar membrane mechanics at the base of the chinchilla cochlea: I. Input–output functions, tuning curves, and response phases. *Journal of the Acoustical Society of America, 80,* 1364–1374.

Sellick, P. M., Patuzzi, R., & Johnstone, B. M. (1982). Measurement of basilar membrane motion in the guinea pig using the Mössbauer technique. *Journal of the Acoustical Society of America, 72,* 131–141.

Shailer, M. J., & Moore, B. C. J. (1983). Gap detection as a function of frequency, bandwidth and level. *Journal of the Acoustical Society of America, 74,* 467–473.

Terhardt, E. (1974). Pitch, consonance, and harmony. *Journal of the Acoustical Society of America, 55,* 1061–1069.

Viemeister, N. F. (1979). Temporal modulation transfer functions based on modulation thresholds. *Journal of the Acoustical Society of America, 66,* 1364–1380.

Vogten, L. L. M. (1974). Pure-tone masking: A new result from a new method. In E. Zwicker & E. Terhardt (Eds) *Facts and models in hearing* (pp. 142–155). Berlin: Springer-Verlag.

von Békésy, G. (1947). The variations of phase along the basilar membrane with sinusoidal vibrations. *Journal of the Acoustical Society of America, 19,* 452–460.

von Békésy, G. (1960). *Experiments in hearing* (E. G. Wever, trans.). New York: McGraw-Hill.

Wallace, H., Newman, E. B., & Rosenzweig, M. R. (1949). The precedence effect in sound localization. *Journal of Experimental Psychology, 27,* 339–368.

Yates, G. K. (1986). Frequency selectivity in the auditory periphery. In B. C. J. Moore (Ed.) *Frequency selectivity in hearing* (pp. 1–50). London: Academic Press.

Yates, G. K. (1990). Basilar membrane nonlinearity and its influence on auditory nerve rate-intensity functions. *Hearing Research, 50,* 145–162.

4

THE SKIN, BODY, AND CHEMICAL SENSES

Harvey Richard Schiffman
Rutgers University, New Jersey, USA

This chapter covers four basic sensory systems: the skin sense, the general body sense, and the related senses of taste and smell. In examining the skin sense we shall deal with how stimulation by touch, temperature, and pain informs about the nature of surfaces and objects that come in contact with our skin. We shall also examine the ability to perceive the spatial position of our limbs and the "sense of balance" – the overall location of the body and head in space. Finally we shall deal with our capacities to taste chemicals when they dissolve in our mouth and stimulate the tongue and to smell gaseous chemicals when they reach our nasal passages.

THE SKIN

The skin of the human, serving both as a sensory organ and a protective surface, is by far the largest organ of the body. It forms a covering for the entire body: a person 6 feet tall, of average weight and body build, possesses about 2 square metres or 3,000 square inches of skin area. The skin is also the most versatile sensory organ of the body, serving as a flexible and renewable shield against many forms of foreign agents, infections, and mechanical injuries. It retains vital body fluids, it wards off harmful solar radiations, it helps to regulate and stabilize internal body temperature by retarding heat loss or cooling the body, and of course, by providing different sensations, the skin informs the organism of what is directly adjacent to the body, especially the presence of potentially harmful stimuli.

The sensory effect of stimulation of the skin is termed *cutaneous sensitivity* and three primary cutaneous qualities have been identified: pressure or touch (also called contact, tactual, or tactile stimulation), temperature (cold or warm), and pain. It has been proposed that the different sensory qualities are mediated by different specialized receptors embedded within the layers of the skin. Some of the proposed receptor types are sketched in Figure 1. The majority of the skin surface is covered with hairs and the presumed major sensory receptors for hairy skin regions are called *basket cells* because they resemble a woven basket wrapped around the bottom of the hair shaft embedded within the inner skin layer. The primary sensory receptors for the much more sparse hairless or *glabrous skin* of the body – certain facial regions including the lips and mouth, palms of the hands, and soles of the feet – are a class of specialized structures called *encapsulated end organs*, which come in a wide variety of forms. The major form embedded in glabrous skin are *Pacinian corpuscles* which have an onion-like appearance (other presumed cutaneous receptors are Meissner's corpuscles and tactile disks for touch, and Ruffini endings for warmth and Krause end bulbs for cold). Additionally, both hairy and hairless skin regions contain receptors called *free nerve endings* that lack specialized receptor cells and are unattached to any specific skin region. Free nerve endings are found almost

71

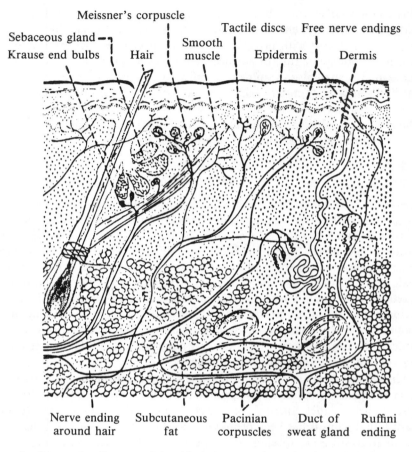

Figure 1 Composite diagram of the skin in cross-section, showing chief layers, epidermis, dermis, and subcutaneous tissue, and a hair follicle and its supporting structures. Also shown are several kinds of nerve endings and receptors that are embedded within the skin
Source: Gardner, 1947, revised from H. R. Schiffman, 1990

everywhere within the skin surface and by far are the most common skin receptor.

All three types of receptors, the basket cells, the Pacininan corpuscles, and the free nerve endings, yield some sort of pressure or touch sensation when stimulated. It thus appears that a given cutaneous pressure sensation may be produced by a number of different specialized receptors in the skin rather than a single one. Moreover it is not clear whether stimulation of a particular type of skin receptor exclusively initiates a specific cutaneous touch sensation. For example, the cornea of the eye contains only free nerve endings but it is very sensitive to pressure, temperature, and pain. It must be concluded that, in general, highly specialized receptors do not appear to be necessary to receive a particular type of stimulus or elicit a specific class of sensation.

It should also be noted that all regions of the skin are not uniformly sensitive to all forms of cutaneous stimulation. Some areas may be sensitive to warm and relatively insensitive to cold stimuli or the reverse; whereas most regions of the skin may be sensitive to pain, different regions may be more sensitive to painful stimulation than others.

Touch and pressure

Touch localization

The skin is extremely sensitive to light pressure. Indeed under ideal conditions, displacements of the skin less than 0.001 mm (0.00004 in.) can result in a sensation of pressure or touch. However, as with thermal and painful stimulation, the sensitivity to touch or pressure stimulation also varies considerably from one region of the body to another. Drawing from common experience we easily recognize that it takes more contact or pressure to feel something on the thigh or the sole of the foot than on the finger tips or on the face. In a classic experiment on a related ability – *point localization* – Weinstein (1968) stimulated observers with fine nylon filaments, to obtain measures of the ability to localize pressure sensations applied to various regions of the skin. As Figure 2 indicates, point localization largely varies with the region of the body stimulated. Since a major function of the skin is to inform the organism of what is directly adjacent to it, it is not surprising that generally, stimulation of the more mobile, exploratory skin regions of the body, endowed with finer muscular control – e.g., the hands and mouth – results in more accurate point localization. For example, stimulation of the fingertip or the lip is extremely well localized, producing an error in the observer's perception of where the stimulus was applied of only about 2 millimetres. In contrast, stimulation of the upper arm, thigh or back produces an error of localization of more than a centimetre.

Two-point threshold

Another means of demonstrating the sensitivity of the skin to touch stimulation is to assess the *two-point threshold*, which refers to the smallest separation of two discrete but adjacent points of stimulation on the skin that just produces two distinct impressions of touch. That is, if they were placed any closer together they would produce a single touch sensation. As with the ability to localize a single stimulus, more mobile regions are more sensitive and have lower two-point thresholds.

73

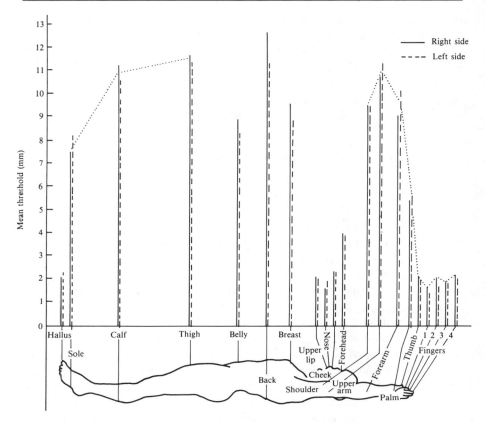

Figure 2 Point localization thresholds. The ordinate represents the distance between the body point stimulated and the observer's judgement of where stimulation occurred

Source: Weinstein, 1968, p. 204. Reproduced by courtesy of Charles C. Thomas, publisher, Springfield, Illinois

Adaptation to touch

It should be noted that continued steady pressure or touch stimulation may result in a decrease or even a complete elimination of a sensation. Clearly even after a short while, we do not usually feel the pressure of our watchband on the wrist or the clothes against our body. That is, touch sensations undergo *adaptation*. The course of adaptation varies with a number of factors, particularly the size, intensity, and the region of the skin under continuous contact. But touch sensations can be quickly restored by some movement or an abrupt change in the stimulation against the skin.

The skin and brain

The efficiency and the variability of the skin in such tasks as point localization and the two-point threshold is highly correlated with the particular skin region's density of nerve fibres and its connection to the brain. Some skin regions such as those of the fingers, lips, and tongue are more densely supplied with nerve fibres; hence, they are more sensitive than other skin areas such as the shoulders; moreover they are correspondingly represented by larger areas in the sensory brain — a cortical region called the *somatosensory cortex* — responsible for receiving and processing touch or pressure stimulation.

The Braille system

The skin, when actively employed, is capable of extracting complex kinds of information from small changes in pressure or touch. One example is the Braille reading system devised by Louis Braille in the nineteenth century. The Braille alphabet is composed of dots embossed on a surface that can be "read" by the skin of the fingertips. As shown in Figure 3, various combinations of dots are used to represent letters and words. By moving the fingertip

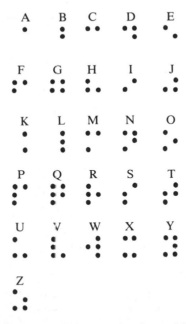

Figure 3 The Braille alphabet. Various combinations of from one to six embossed dots are used to represent letters and short words. Each dot is raised 1 mm above the surface and the dot separations are 2.3 mm

over the raised surface of Braille writing, the experienced adult Braille reader can reach 100 words or more per minute (e.g., Kennedy, 1984).

The Tadoma method

The Braille system enables a blind individual to "read" with the skin. Touch may also be used by some individuals who are both blind and deaf to communicate speech by using the *Tadoma* method of speech reception (Loomis & Lederman, 1986; Reed, Dohrty, Braida, & Durlach, 1982). In the Tadoma method the "listener" places his or her hand in contact with specific parts of the speaker's lips, jaw and neck so that the hand receives some of the complex patterns of vibration stimulation in the airflow and lip and jaw movements produced by the speaker's vocalizations (see Figure 4). If the rate of speech is slow, use of the Tadoma system permits a well-experienced "listener" to reach a modest but useful level of speech comprehension.

Tactile visual substitution system

While we have outlined only two kinds of information extracted from touch stimulation it should be clear that on the basis of touch alone it is possible

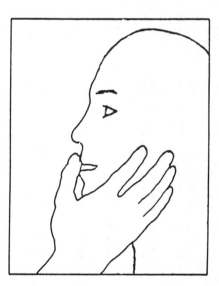

Figure 4 Hand placement using the Tadoma method of speech perception. As the speaker talks the "listener" can directly pick up information that is closely tied to articulation, such as oral air flow and lip and jaw movement
Source: Revised from Loomis and Lederman, 1986, based on Reed, Doherty, Braida, and Durlach, 1982

to perceive complex and spatially detailed forms of environmental stimulation. Indeed it is possible to convert a visual image into a direct tactual display on the skin by using a technology called the *Tactile visual substitution system*. Specifically, a video camera records a scene containing an array of objects; then the image of the scene is electronically transformed and reproduced into a succession of vibratory impressions on the skin surface (usually the back). With experience, especially when they can control the scanning pattern of the video camera, observers are able to interpret the pattern of stimulations as representing specific objects, and they can even perceive the location of objects relative to each other within a spatial framework. The authors of this technology appropriately term this functional use of tactual stimulation, "seeing with the skin" (White, Saunders, Scadden, Bach-y-Rita, & Collins, 1970).

Tactual stereognosis

Finally, in this context of the meaningful extraction of environmental information from touch, we must take note of the phenomenon of tactual *stereognosis*, the familiar and extremely accurate ability to perceive three-dimensional shapes by palpation or manipulation by the hands. Indeed, almost effortlessly we can identify objects solely on the basis of how they "feel". In one investigation, Klatsky, Lederman, and Metzger (1985) studied the ability of blindfolded subjects to identify common objects solely by feeling them. The subjects handled 100 common objects, each easily identifiable by name, for example, a paper clip, toothbrush, fork, and screwdriver. The results were impressive with respect to the subjects' accuracy and overall competence in palpation: out of a total of 2,000 judgements, approximately 96 per cent were correct and 94 per cent of the correct judgements occurred within 5 seconds of handling the object.

Temperature

The sensations resulting from the temperature of a surface that is in contact with the skin is also registered by a form of cutaneous stimulation. The surface of the skin is irregularly distributed with spots that are thermally sensitive, some spots more sensitive to warm, other spots more sensitive to cold stimulation.

Adaptation to temperature

As with constant pressure or touch stimulation, thermal sensations from the skin undergo adaptation. Exposure to a moderately warm or cold environment, as in the case of entering a bath or swimming pool, may initially result in a very warm or cold experience, but despite a constant thermal environment, eventually the thermal sensations diminish and the water feels only slightly warm or cool, respectively. Moreover, with prolonged immersion in the warm or cold thermal environment adaptation may be total in which case no thermal sensation may occur until there is a change in its temperature.

Generally the skin surface is adapted to a narrow range of temperatures which fails to yield a warm or cold sensation – a neutral zone of complete thermal adaptation – called *physiological zero*. Normally, physiological zero corresponds to the temperature of the skin which is about 91°F (33°C). That is, temperatures applied to the skin that are close to 91°F feel neither warm

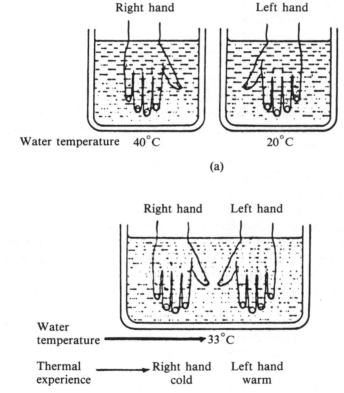

Right hand   Left hand

Water temperature   40°C   20°C

(a)

Right hand   Left hand

Water
temperature ⟶ 33°C

Thermal ⟶ Right hand   Left hand
experience   cold   warm

(b)

Figure 5 Effects of thermal adaptation. (a) Each hand is placed in a separate basin of water and is thermally adapted to a different temperature. (b) When both hands are then placed in the 33°C water, the right hand, previously adapted to warm water, feels cold, and the left hand, previously adapted to cold water, feels warm. These sensory effects of thermal adaptation point out that the skin is not a good indicator of physical temperature
Source: Based on H. R. Schiffman, 1990

78

nor cold (the neutral zone usually extends 2–4°C to either side of physiological zero). But it should be noted that physiological zero can occur with a number of temperatures. A demonstration attributed to John Locke in 1690 makes this point and also points out that the skin is not a good indicator of physical temperature. As outlined in Figure 5, one hand is immersed in a 40°C basin of water, and the other in a 20°C basin and both are allowed to thermally adapt until neither hand feels any thermal sensation. If then both hands are then shifted in to a 33°C basin of water, the water in the 33°C basin will now feel distinctly cold to the hand that was originally in the warm water and warm to the hand that was originally in the cold water. As shown in Figure 5, owing to prior thermal adaptation, the same physical temperature can feel cold to one hand and warm to the other. Thus thermal sensations occur as a result of the relation of the temperature of the skin surface to the temperature of its surroundings rather than from the reception of absolute physical temperature itself.

Pain

It is clear that towards the extremes of thermal stimulation – freezing and boiling – thermal sensations merge with those of pain. This is a biologically adaptive association because intense thermal stimulation can produce tissue damage. Since painful stimuli, in general, are immediately attended to, this helps protect the organism against harmful and even lethal thermal extremes.

Although we recognize that tissue injury is neither a necessary nor a sufficient condition for the experience of pain, generally speaking, most forms of painful stimuli are potentially damaging. Thus a significant benefit from the reception of pain is warning of potential biological harm. Indeed chronic failure to perceive pain is extremely maladaptive: the pernicious physical effects occurring to individuals who lack the sense of pain provide convincing evidence of its overall value to the organism's well-being. Reports of self-inflicted injury due to pathological pain insensitivity, especially in childhood, have included serious, often life-threatening, injury to the skin, flesh, and bones, extensive burns from hot surfaces and liquids, and even chewing off the tip of the tongue (e.g., Melzack, 1973).

The nociceptor

It is generally held that pain results from the excitation of a specialized receptor called a *nociceptor* (from the Latin *nocere*, "to injure"). A nociceptor is a receptor that is activated by stimulation that may produce injury to the body and whose sensations are unpleasant. For a number of reasons, but most importantly because they are found wherever pain spots are located, free nerve ending receptors (introduced earlier) are generally assumed to be nociceptors.

Variability in pain perception

It is worth noting that pain is not a single sensation produced by a single or specific stimulus; rather pain may encompass a range of different, unpleasant experiences produced by a wide variety of potentially harmful, noxious events. Moreover, a rather remarkable aspect of pain perception is its extremely variable relationship to the stimulus that elicits it. Indeed the relation between pain and bodily injury extends from injury with no pain to extreme pain with little or no injury. A pain stimulus that is experienced as extreme in one situation may not be so in another. Among the psychological factors that affect this variability in perceiving pain is one's emotional state and level of stress. Thus severe injuries sustained in competitive sports and combat may be accompanied by little or no pain. Clearly there are numerous cognitive, social and cultural factors that markedly affect pain perception. Indeed it is often the case that the same injury produces different effects in different individuals.

Melzack (1973) describes several culturally based initiation rites and rituals (of India and of the North American Plains Indians) that involve suspending and swinging "celebrants" by skewers and hooks that are inserted into their chests and backs as part of religious ceremony. Rather than showing the effects of pain, the celebrants appear more in a state of exaltation and ecstasy. That variability in pain perception may be linked to culture is further supported by some clinical observations following major surgery. One orthopaedic surgeon (cited in H. R. Schiffman, 1990, p. 147), reported that he had performed spinal grafts or fusions (in which bone fragments are chipped from regions of the pelvic bone and placed over vertebrae) on Canadian Indians on one day, and on the next day they walked about as if without any pain. Such stoic behaviour was never observed with members of other cultural groups who underwent the same surgical procedure.

The spinal gate control theory

There are specific pathways to the brain that signal pain. As we noted, free nerve endings are the likely receptors – the nociceptors – for pain in the skin. They are linked to specific fibres connecting to the spinal cord, which in turn contains neurons that also react selectively to noxious stimuli. However, as we noted above, sometimes an environmental event that is usually experienced as painful is barely sensed at all. That is, pain sensation is a highly variable experience. Melzack and Wall (1965, 1982; see also Morris, 1991) have proposed a comprehensive theory that they called the *spinal gate control theory* to explain the general mechanism of pain perception; it also takes into account why pain perception is so variable. Their basic idea is that there is a neural "gate" in the spinal cord that can be opened or closed to allow or inhibit painful stimulation to be sent, by way of specific transmission (T) cells, from the spinal cord to the brain along the specific pain pathways. According to the spinal gate control theory, three interlocking factors control the opening and closing of the spinal gate and the transmission of T cell activity. First, when pain receptors of the skin are sufficiently stimulated, they activate the T cells in the spinal cord which signals the presence of painful stimulation. That is, activity of nociceptors "opens" the spinal gate and increases the sensation of pain. Second, when nociceptor activity (i.e., pain or nociceptor stimulation) is also accompanied by excitations from skin receptors that carry messages concerning non-painful cutaneous stimulation – such as from light touch and stroking of the skin – activity of the pain receptors are inhibited and T cell activity of the spinal cord accordingly decreases. That is, excitation of certain touch-sensitive receptors of the skin "closes" the spinal gate and decreases the sensation of pain. In this case, the neural activity of non-painful stimuli competes with and displaces the neural message from nociceptor activity, thereby reducing the pain sensation. This helps explain why sometimes gently stroking or rubbing the skin around the site of an injury helps reduce the pain, or why scratching is able to briefly relieve an itch (which is a kind of low-grade pain stimulus): such activity stimulates pressure-sensitive receptors and partly closes the spinal gate.

The third factor that exerts control on the spinal gate is a central-cognitive mechanism from the brain itself. Neurons in the brain have pathways back to the spinal cord and by this route can send a message down the spinal cord and close the spinal gate, thus inhibiting the activity of the T cells. It follows that since messages originating from the brain can affect the spinal gate, psychological factors such as stress and emotion, attention and attitude, and other cognitive factors can also exert control over T cell activity and thereby affect pain sensation.

The spinal gate control theory is consistent with a number of phenomena involving pain suppression by cutaneous stimulation. For example, there is evidence that selectively transmitting non-painful touch stimulation such as occurs with therapeutically massaging an injured region or the application of low-intensity electrical pulses – experienced as "tingling" – can reduce chronic cutaneous pain. The spinal gate control theory may also explain the effectiveness as a pain suppressor of *acupuncture*, an ancient Chinese technique in which needles are inserted into various parts of the body. It has been proposed that the needles, when heated, twirled or electrified, send non-painful cutaneous excitations that close the presumed spinal gate.

Endorphins

There is considerable evidence that the body produces natural pain suppressors called *endorphins*. Endorphins are neurotransmitter chemicals manufactured by the body that interact with a particular kind of neuron called an opiate receptor. Opiate receptors act to reduce pain sensation, and in fact, many pain-reducing drugs, especially the opiate drugs (derivatives of opium such as morphine), are specifically administered to stimulate the opiate receptors. Of course, opiate receptors in the body did not evolve to react specifically to opiates or other substances foreign to the body. Rather, it is most likely that the function of opiate receptors is to mediate the body's own capacity to reduce pain. Endorphins (the word is a contraction of "endogenous morphine") are thus chemicals produced by the body itself and serve a biologically significant role in pain management and control.

The clearest evidence for activation of an endogenous pain reducing mechanism comes from animal studies in which unrelenting stress or pain stimulation is applied (e.g., Bolles & Fanselow, 1982; Grau, 1984; Terman, Shavit, Lewis, Cannon, & Liebeskind, 1984). The existence of a human endorphin mechanism is generally accepted, but direct evidence is scarce (Bandura, O'Leary, Taylor, Gauthier, & Gossard, 1987). Of interest to the preceding discussion on the spinal gate control mechanism, is that the spinal cord is highly enriched in opiate receptors. Perhaps endorphins act by inhibiting the release of excitatory substances for neurons carrying information about pain. That is, endorphins may "close" the spinal gate and thereby suppress pain.

THE BODY SENSES

Thus far we have concentrated on the awareness of the environment that surrounds us when contact is made with our skin. However, there is also an immense amount of vital information generated within our bodies. This class of information informs us of such things as the position and movement of our mobile body parts, and it tells us whether we are tilted or erect and whether we are in transit or stationary. There are two sensory mechanisms for receiving and monitoring this kind of information called *kinaesthesis* and the *vestibular sense*.

Kinaesthesis

Kinaesthesis refers to the sensory system that receives and processes information about the posture, location, and movement in space of the limbs and other mobile parts of the jointed skeleton. The sensory mechanism for kinaesthesis makes use of receptors that reside within the joints, muscles, and tendons. The proposed receptors for the joints are *Pacinian corpuscles* (similar to those we encountered within the skin); these lie in the mobile joints of the skeletal system and they are stimulated by mechanical contact between the parts of the joints' surfaces. That is, stimulation of the Pacinian corpuscles occurs with changes in the angles at which the bones of a joint are held relative to each other. In addition, muscles and their attached tendons are well supplied with sensory nerves that react to changes in tension when the muscle fibre is stretched or contracted. Thus with movement of the limbs in space the brain receives information concerning joint movement and the state of muscle tension.

Clearly, the kinaesthetic system provides a source of critical bodily information. Effortlessly, we are aware of, and continuously monitor the position, posture, and the direction of the movement of our limbs in space. Thus we easily scratch an itch that we cannot see, and we walk safely down a flight of steps without gazing directly at our feet.

The vestibular sense

The kinaesthetic information provided by the joints, muscles, and tendons enables the brain to know where the various body parts are relative to one another. Thus being aware of the angles of the toes, ankles, knees, hips, shoulders, and so on, enables an individual to distinguish a crouch from an upright position or from standing on one's tiptoes. Similarly, sensing the angles of the wrist, hand, and finger joints, allows the brain to recognize whether the hand is holding a small or a large object. However, such information does not tell the brain the position of the body, or how it moves with regard to the environment or to gravity. In order to obtain this sort of information the brain requires an additional class of position information.

Saccule and utricle

Awareness of body position, equilibrium, and movement in space arises from the two *vestibular* structures that lie within the inner ear. The first vestibular structure is comprised of two small sacs, the *saccule* and the *utricle*, which are attached to the auditory structures of the inner ear (see Figure 6). These two vestibular sacs are lined with hair-like, *cilia* receptors that are covered with extremely small calcium crystals. When you are relatively stationary and stand upright the force of gravity forces downward movement of the calcium crystals and bends the cilia lining the bottom surface of the sacs; when you abruptly move your head, such as when jumping downward, the mass of calcium particles lags somewhat because of inertial forces, thus bending the cilia lining the top surface of the sacs. In fact, any sort of linear movement bends and excites specific cilia producing a consequent discharge of attached nerve fibres and sends an appropriate message to the brain. Thus in a very real sense the saccule and utricle serve as gravity detectors and inform an individual which way is "up" and which way is "down". They also signal *changes* in movement (i.e., linear acceleration or deceleration) of the body, such as changes in up and down, forward and backward, or side to side movement: that is, they react to starts and stops and changes in motion, as opposed to sustained movement at a constant velocity.

83

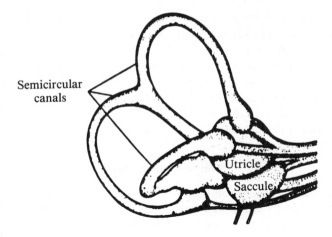

Semicircular
canals

Figure 6 The vestibular organs, showing the utricle, saccule, and three semicircular
canals
Source: Based on H. R. Schiffman, 1990

Semicircular canals

The second vestibular structure is actually a set of three fluid-filled canals –
called the *semicircular canals* – set at approximately right angles to each
other (see Figure 6). The primary function of the canals is to register information of angular acceleration or rotation of the head. Each canal relates to
a major plane of the body and when stimulated during rotation of the head,
the fluid in the canals moves in relation to the direction and extent of the
rotary changes. Displacement of the fluid within the canals excites specific
receptors that lie within the canals and corresponding signals of the direction
of the rotation are sent to the brain. Thus collectively, the semicircular canals
form a three-coordinate system to which the direction of head rotation can
be referred.

The vestibular system performs vital functions, providing information
concerning gravity and linear and rotary movement, and accordingly assists
in the maintenance of an upright posture. Another function performed by the
vestibular sense is to help stabilize vision by coordinating eye and head position. As we move about through the spatial environment, our head bobs and
weaves continuously. To adjust for changes in the visual imagery due to the
continual head movement, the eyes have to move accordingly. The compen-
sation for the visual changes is accomplished by a complex reflex system that
automatically and smoothly compensates for each head movement by an
equal and opposite movement of the eyes. Thus, for example, if you lock
your gaze at something in the environment while turning your head to the
left, your eyes will move to the right and the visual image of what you have
fixated on remains stabilized. These automatic compensatory eye movements

are initiated by neural signals from the vestibular system to the brain which are relayed to the muscles of the eyes that control their movement. The perceptual result, of course, is that as we move about, the visual scene appears stabilized and fixed on the retina.

Motion sickness

The vestibular system is well-suited to receive stimulation that is typically self-produced by individuals who move about in a three-dimensional environment, subject to the earth's gravity. However, when we take advantage of some of the opportunities provided by passive vehicular transport, such as with ships, cars, trains, and aircraft, we may introduce abnormal motion stimulation that the vestibular sense cannot effectively deal with, and the result is *motion sickness*. Motion sickness is a widespread phenomenon that can be totally disabling, usually accompanied by pallor, dizziness and vertigo, and nausea. A major explanation of motion sickness is that it is the result of a conflict between the main sources of sensory information about the spatial orientation of the head and body (e.g., Young, 1984). That is, the moment-to-moment position information signalled by the visual sense is discrepant or mismatched with that signalled by the vestibular sense. For example, when you are in the cabin of a ship that is in choppy waters, your vestibular sense signals the erratic series of movements that are imposed on your body, while your visual sense signals a relatively stable visual environment. Perhaps more familiar is the strong reaction to reading a book while in a moving vehicle, especially when moving over a bumpy road. In such conditions it is the *conflict* between the visual signals and the passively imposed vestibular signals that produces the motion sickness. To some extent the symptoms of motion sickness may be relieved or reduced if the information provided by the visual sense is made somewhat consistent with the vestibular stimulation. In our sea example, this could be attempted by looking at the rough water and anticipating the movements of the ship (and one's body); but even here the series of abnormal, passively imposed motion signals is often too much of a challenge to the vestibular system for anything but a moderate reduction in the distress experienced.

THE CHEMICAL SENSES: TASTE AND SMELL

Both taste (technically, *gustation*) and smell (*olfaction*) depend on receptors that are normally stimulated by chemical substances, and these receptors are called *chemoreceptors*. Aside from the fact that they both require chemical stimuli, taste and smell are functionally linked. Their close relationship can be easily demonstrated. If the reception for smell is reduced or eliminated by blockage of the air passages of the nose, such as by tightly pinching the nostrils, or as sometimes happens to a person who has caught a common cold (in which an overproduction of mucous results in a congestion of the olfactory sensory cells), two quite different food substances may taste surprisingly similar. For example, under such conditions of reduced smell, raw potato does not taste very different from apple. What this points out, of course, is that many of the "taste" qualities that are ordinarily assigned to foods are in fact due to their odours (Moncrieff, 1951). Moreover it is clear that together, taste and smell interact as a functional unit serving in many dietary activities, such as food seeking and sampling, and ingesting or rejecting substances. However, it is equally clear that taste and smell also possess quite independent functions: thus for many forms of animal life, smell enables the reception of non-nutritive information such as detecting the presence of prey or predator and it is critical for sexual activity, whereas taste aids in the regulation of nutrients, enabling an organism's tongue and mouth to test or "sample" substances prior to ingestion. Accordingly, while we recognize that taste and smell are closely allied senses, for the most part, we shall here treat each sense separately.

Taste

The chemical stimulus

A potential stimulus for taste must be a dissolved or soluble substance that must go into solution on coming in contact with saliva, a requirement that limits taste to water-soluble molecules. For the human there are four basic or primary tastes: sweet, sour, salty, and bitter. Presently there are no precise or exact rules to specify the taste of a substance based on its chemical composition. However, it is generally the case that the salty taste comes from organic salts, especially table salt or sodium chloride (NaCl), the sour taste from acid compounds, the sweet taste from nutrients associated with organic substances such as carbohydrates and amino acids, and the bitter taste from alkaloids (which are usually poisonous). The observation that nutritive substances tend to be sweet, and poisonous substances tend to be bitter, strongly suggests that the ability to sense sweet and bitter is necessary for survival. Likewise a salt taste has a vital adaptive function, playing a unique role in the regulation of body fluid. With insufficient salt we cannot retain water, blood volume plummets, and the heart fails. Indeed as we sometimes recognize in our own dietary activities, a critical loss of sodium stimulates a strong craving for salty foods. It should be noted further that the salt taste also warns against the ingestion of intolerably high concentrations of salt, which can have as serious consequences to the normal functioning of the body as does insufficient salt. Thus we may accept as a very general rule, at least for most naturally occurring substances, that things that have an unpleasant taste are likely to be harmful or even poisonous and usually indigestible, whereas substances that are appealing are likely to be necessary for the metabolism and homeostasis of the body.

Receptors for taste

The basic receptors for taste in the human, called *taste buds*, are specialized structures located in microscopically small pits and grooves throughout the oral cavity but particularly on the surface of the tongue (see Figure 7). A taste bud is composed of taste cells that have finger-like projections called *microvilli* which extend into taste pores and are in direct contact with saliva and chemical solutions applied to the surface of the tongue. The human possesses about 10,000 taste buds, which are generally found in clusters lying within small, but visible elevations on the tongue, called *papillae*.

The tongue and taste sensitivity

Not all papillae are equally responsive to the basic tastes. That is, different regions of the tongue are more sensitive to specific taste stimuli than are others. Figure 8 shows the regional differences in taste sensitivity. The front of the tongue is most sensitive to the sweet taste, the back sides for sour, the front and sides of the tongue are most sensitive to the salt taste, and the front (and especially the soft palate) is most sensitive to bitter. However, it should be noted that although they are not equally sensitive, all areas of the tongue respond to almost all of the basic tastes. Indeed, studies in which sweet, bitter, sour, and salty stimuli were applied to individual taste buds indicate

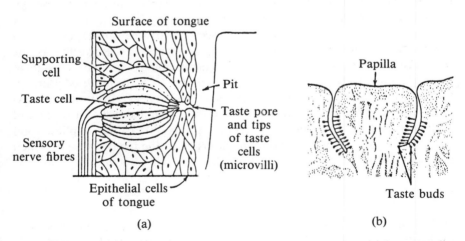

Figure 7 (a) Drawing of a taste bud. Sensory nerve fibres connect to the taste cells; the tips of the taste cells project microvilli into the taste pore. (b) Clusters of taste buds form papillae

Source: Based on H. R. Schiffman, 1990

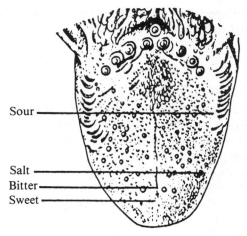

Figure 8 Approximate location on the tongue of regions of greatest taste sensitivities for the four primary taste qualities. For the bitter taste, the soft palate (not shown) is the most sensitive region
Source: Based on data from Collings, 1974

that, with sufficient concentration, a single taste bud will react to more than one taste stimulus (Arvidson & Friberg, 1980; Collings, 1974).

Temperature and taste

Taste sensitivity for a substance is affected not only by its chemical composition but also by a wide variety of stimulus variables, such as its concentration, the area of its application, the age, species, and prior dietary conditions of the taster, and the temperature of the substance. As an example, consider how temperature affects taste sensitivity. Regardless of the basic taste quality of a substance, taste sensitivity is greatest for substances when they are between 22°C and 32°C (about 72°F to 90°F; McBurney, Collings, & Glanz, 1973). This corresponds with the generalization that maximal sensitivity to most compounds occurs in the range between room and body temperature. In general, of course, the cook's caveat applies: food seasoning – salt or sugar – should be adjusted at the temperature at which the food will be served.

Taste adaptation

If the tongue is continually stimulated with an identical solution, sensitivity to that taste declines quickly and may eventually be completely lacking. This decrement in taste sensitivity is due to *adaptation*, an effect of unchanging stimulation that is observed in virtually every sensory modality. For example, after a period of constant stimulation with a bitter solution such as with strong caffeinated black coffee, the bitter taste of the coffee becomes weaker and weaker and may eventually appear tasteless. However, if the coffee is rinsed out and the mouth left unstimulated for a short while, taste sensitivity to coffee is restored in full, thereby reversing the adaptation process.

Adaptation to one taste stimulus can also affect the taste of a different taste stimulus. An unusual example of this is the effect that adaptation to certain substances has on the taste of water. If, for example, your tongue is well adapted to the bitter taste of strong black coffee, a taste of distilled water will taste slightly sweet. Similarly, adaptation to a sweet solution will impart a bitter taste to water. This phenomenon of taste induction has been termed *adaptation-produced potentiation*; it has been shown that each of the four primary tastes can be imparted to water by prior adaptation to certain chemical solutions (McBurney & Shick, 1971).

Conditioned taste aversion

When individuals are exposed − even once − to a substance accompanied by certain unpleasant conditions such as nausea, a powerful and relatively long-lasting aversion to that substance may be created (Garcia, Hankins, & Rusiniak, 1974). The phenomenon is called *conditioned taste aversion* and it is of considerable theoretical and practical interest to psychologists because it shows how a very strong association can be formed after only a single pairing of a stimulus (taste) and a response (sickness). Individuals with a conditioned taste aversion to a food avoid the offending food not so much because they assume that sickness will follow its ingestion but because the food seems to acquire an unpleasant taste.

A serious consequence to conditioned taste aversion, observed with cancer patients undergoing radiation and chemotherapy treatment (which also induces nausea and sickness), is that the patients often acquire taste aversions for foods consumed close to the time of the therapy (Bernstein & Webster, 1980). Accordingly it is advisable that attention be paid to the kind of food consumed close to treatment since long-lasting aversions may develop with any ingested substance, even highly favoured ones.

Smell

The chemical stimulus

In order for a substance to be smelled it must be *volatile*, that is, it must readily vaporize and pass into a gaseous state. In general, the typical chemical stimuli for the olfactory sense are organic substances, usually mixtures of chemical compounds such as the odours emitted by vegetative life, decaying matter, and the scent-producing glands of animals. However, unlike the taste sense there is no agreed upon set of primary odour qualities and the number of distinct odours is immense. Moreover the relationship between the physical and chemical properties of a stimulus and the odour that it arouses is far from clear. In short, there is little agreement about the underlying mechanism that makes specific chemicals excite olfactory receptors and arouse a particular odour. However, it is generally held that a specific set of receptors is *not* exclusively excited by specific chemicals – such as say, a specific set of receptors reacting only to chemicals that we label as "fragrant" and another set of receptors reacting only to chemicals that we label as "spicy", and so on. Instead, it is proposed that the specific neural code for odour quality is based on a *pattern* or response profile of excitations across a number of different receptors; that is, the same olfactory receptors respond to different chemical stimuli but in different ways. In turn, the particular code of neural activity for a particular odour is sent to the olfactory centres of the brain.

Receptors for smell

The sense of smell begins with the inhalation of airborne molecules into the nasal cavity, which then stimulate receptors cells located in the upper reaches of the passages. Figure 9 presents an outline of the main olfactory structures. Although it is not clear how the molecules actually excite the receptor cells,

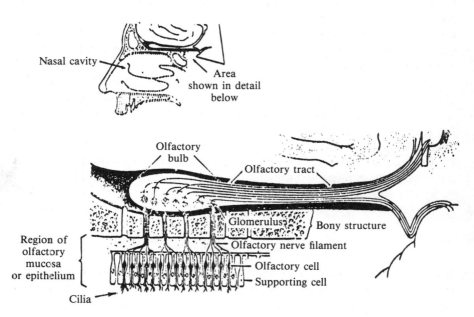

Figure 9 Schematic of anatomy of olfactory system and detail of its cellular structure
Source: Based on H. R. Schiffman, 1990

stimulation probably occurs when the gaseous molecules interact with small cilia on the receptor cells.

Sensitivity of smell

The olfactory system is remarkably sensitive to minute amounts of certain odorants. Indeed, as Mozell (1971) points out, the olfactory system can detect the presence of a smaller number of molecules than can most laboratory methods used for the same purpose. A striking example of this is provided by our sensitivity to *mercaptan*, a foul-smelling compound often added to odorless natural gas as a warning signal of its presence: a concentration of one part of mercaptan per 50 trillion parts of air is detectable (Geldard, 1972, p. 448). Clearly, with respect to the concentration of molecules, smell is the more sensitive of the chemical senses — 10,000 times as sensitive as taste, according to Moncrieff (1951). Even so, the human is much less sensitive to certain odours than are other animals. For example, the average dog possesses a much keener sense of smell than does the average human. The reason is that dogs (and many other mammals) possess many times the olfactory receptors than does the human.

It should be noted in this context that there are differences in sensitivity that are gender and age related. Specifically, females are more sensitive to certain odours than are males. The threshold for Exaltolide, a musk-like synthetic odorant used as a fixative in perfume, is 1,000 times lower for sexually mature women than for males (Doty, Snyder, Huggins, & Lowry, 1981; Vierling & Rock, 1967). In a series of studies, mature males were either *anosmic* (i.e., lacking a sense of smell) to Exaltolide, or barely perceived it (Good, Geary, & Engen, 1976; Vierling & Rock, 1967). It is worth noting here also that there is evidence indicating that females outperform males in the identification as well as the detection of many odours (Doty et al., 1984). In spite of this, the "noses" who work (for only about two hours a day) in French perfume factories are generally men.

While sensitivity to taste shows only a moderate decrease with age, particularly for the sweet and salt taste, overall sensitivity to smell markedly decreases with age (S. S. Schiffman, Moss, & Erickson, 1976). In one study the average ability to identify odours was greatest for individuals between 20 and 40 years and declined markedly thereafter (Doty et al., 1984; Murphy, 1987). It was further observed that 25 per cent of the people tested between the ages of 65 and 68, and nearly 50 per cent of the people tested over the age of 80 years were anosmic, that is, insensitive to odours. Of some interest here is the finding that, at all ages tested, non-smokers outperform smokers on tasks requiring the detection and identification of odours.

Adaptation

As with the other senses, the sense of smell is subject to adaptation; that is, continued exposure to an odorant results in a decline in sensitivity to it. Depending on the particular odour and its concentration, with a sufficient exposure duration, the smell of the odour is almost eliminated (Cain, 1988). Olfactory adaptation is a commonplace experience. Owing to adaptation we are usually not aware of our own objectionable body odours (although we may be painfully aware of the odours of other individuals). Similarly the cooking odours one initially senses when entering the kitchen seem to be gone after a period of continued exposure.

Identification of odours

The human appears to be able to identify certain important characteristics of odours. For example, in studies of odour recognition, women were able to identify their own babies solely on the basis of smell just a few hours after birth (Porter, Balogh, Cernoch, & Franchi, 1986; Porter, Cernoch, & McLaughlin, 1983); newborn babies could discriminate the odour of their own mother's breast and milk from those of a strange mother (Russell, 1976). Russell reported that observers could accurately identify the gender of wearers of undershirts worn for 24 hours by individuals who neither bathed nor used any deodorant or perfume; that is, identification was based on the wearers' perspiration. Similarly, Wallace (1977) found that observers could discriminate males from females with over 80 per cent accuracy by smelling only the perspiration from the person's hand. In addition to the odour of perspiration, Doty, Green, Ram, & Yankell (1982) found that observers were moderately successful in judging a person's gender solely on the basis of his or her breath. Consistent with an earlier point made, females outperformed males on all these tasks.

Memory of odours

Odours have a remarkable capacity to call up long-ago events and memories. However, sometimes they seem to evoke only vague feelings and memories that we feel certain we experienced before, but at the same time we are unsure what they were and when they occurred. This occasional tendency to recognise that an odour is familiar combined with the inability to identify its source is called the *tip-of-the-nose* phenomenon (Lawless & Engen, 1977). Indeed, a striking aspect of our memory of odours is that although the initial identification and recognition of odours is only moderate – not nearly as high as our memory for many visual materials such as pictures – the memories of odours, especially those associated with real-life experiences are quite long lasting. In one experiment on this phenomenon, Engen and Ross (1973) reported that when subjects were given a diverse set of 20 odours of familiar household products, they recognised only about 70 per cent when tested immediately after exposure. However, when tested one year later the average recognition score had dropped only about 5 per cent, indicating that odour memory shows little loss over time (see also Engen, 1987; Shepard, 1967).

Pheromones

For many animals smell provides an important mode of communication. By releasing *pheromones*, complex odorous chemicals that produce specific reactions in other members of the same species, they are able to send such messages as species and colony recognition, sexual arousal and availability, mark scent trails and territorial boundaries. There are two main types of pheromones. *Primers* produce physiological changes such as altering hormonal activity thereby affecting an animal's reproductive cycle and its sexual receptivity. *Releasers* automatically trigger an immediate behavioural response in an animal. They can serve as powerful sexual stimulants that attract sexual partners for the receptive member. Among the more familiar effects of a releaser pheromone in mammals is the female dog in heat attracting mates. Another familiar example of pheromonal activity is the domesticated male cat spraying around the borders of a room marking his territory.

Evidence of pheromonally elicited behaviour in the human is speculative at best. Studies indicate that women who are close friends or who live together tend to have menstrual cycles that are closely synchronized (Graham & McGrew, 1980; McClintock, 1971, 1984; Quadagno, Shubeita, Deck, & Francoeur 1981). There is also supporting evidence that olfactory cues promote the menstrual synchrony (McClintock, 1984; Russell, Switz, & Thompson, 1980) and that the volatile chemicals influencing the timing of menstrual activity are found in human perspiration (Cutler et al., 1986; Preti et al., 1986). However, the functional implications of the odour's influence on human physiology remains unknown.

FURTHER READING

Engen, T. (1987). Remembering odors and their names. *American Scientist*, 75, 497–503.

Finger, T. E., & Silver, W. L. (Eds) (1987). *Neurobiology of taste and smell*. New York: Wiley.

Howard, I. P. (1982). *Human visual orientation*. New York: Wiley.

Klatsky, R. L., Lederman, S. J., & Metzger, V. A. (1985). Identifying objects by touch: An "expert system". *Perception and Psychophysics*, 37, 200–302.

Schiffman, H. R. (1990). *Sensation and perception: An integrated approach*. New York: Wiley.

REFERENCES

Arvidson, K., & Friberg, U. (1980). Human taste: Response and taste bud number in fungiform papillae. *Science, 209*, 806–807.

Bandura, A., O'Leary, A., Taylor, C. B., Gauthier, J., & Gossard, D. (1987). Perceived self-efficacy and pain control: Opioid and nonopioid mechanisms. *Journal of Personality and Social Psychology, 53*, 563–571.

Bernstein, I. L., & Webster, M. M. (1980). Learned taste aversions in humans. *Physiology and Behavior, 25*, 363–366.

Bolles, R. C., & Fanselow, M. S. (1982). Endorphins and behavior. *Annual Review of Psychology, 33*, 87–101.

Cain, W. S. (1988). Olfaction. In R. C. Atkinson, R. J. Herrnstein, G. Lindzey, & R. D. Luce (Eds) *Stevens' handbook of experimental psychology* (2nd edn, vol. 1, pp. 409–459). New York: Wiley.

Collings, V. B. (1974). Human taste response as a function of locus of stimulation on the tongue and soft palate. *Perception and Psychophysics, 16*, 169–174.

Cutler, W. B., Preti, G., Krieger, A., Huggins, G. R., Garcia, C. R., & Lawley, H. J. (1986). Human axillary secretions influence women's menstrual cycles: The role of donor extract from men. *Hormones and Behavior, 20*, 463–473.

Doty, R. L., Snyder, P. J., Huggins, G. R., & Lowry, L. D. (1981). Endocrine, cardiovascular and psychological correlates of olfactory sensitivity changes during the human menstrual cycle. *Journal of Comparative and Physiological Psychology, 95*, 45–60.

Doty, R. L., Green, P. A., Ram, C., & Yankell, S. L. (1982). Communication of gender from human breath odors: Relationship to perceived intensity and pleasantness. *Hormones and Behavior, 16*, 13–22.

Doty, R. L., Shaman, P., Applebaum, S. L., Gilberson, R., Sikorski, L., & Rosenberg, L. (1984). Smell identification ability: Changes with age. *Science, 226*, 1441–1444.

Engen, T. (1987). Remembering odors and their names. *American Scientist, 75*, 497–503.

Engen, T., & Ross, B. M. (1973). Long-term memory of odors with and without verbal descriptions. *Journal of Experimental Psychology, 100*, 221–227.

Garcia, J., Hankins W. G., & Rusiniak, K. W. (1974). Behavioral regulation of the milieu interne in man and rat. *Science, 185*, 824–831.

Gardner, E. (1947). *Fundamentals of neurology.* Philadelphia, PA: Saunders.

Geldard, F. A. (1972). *The human senses* (2nd edn). New York: Wiley.

Good, P. R., Geary, N., & Engen, T. (1976). The effect of estrogen on odor detection. *Chemical Senses and Flavor, 2*, 45–50.

Graham, C. A., & McGraw, W. C. (1980). Menstrual synchrony in female undergraduates living on a coeducational campus. *Psychoneuroendocrinology, 5*, 245–252.

Grau, J. W. (1984). Influence of naloxone on shock-induced freezing and analgesia. *Behavioral Neuroscience, 98*, 278–292.

Howard, I. P. (1982). *Human visual orientation.* New York: Wiley.

Kennedy, J. M. (1984). The tangible world of the blind. *Encyclopaedia Britannica Medical and Health Annual.* Chicago, IL: Encyclopaedia Britannica.

Kenshalo, D. R. (Ed.) (1968). *The skin senses.* Springfield, IL: Charles C. Thomas.

Klatsky, R. L., Lederman, S. J., & Metzger, V. A. (1985). Identifying objects by touch: An "expert system". *Perception and Psychophysics, 37*, 200–302.

Lawless H. T., & Engen, T. (1977). Associations to odors: Interference, mnemonics, and verbal labels. *Journal of Experimental Psychology: Human Learning and Memory, 3*, 52–59.

Loomis, J. M., & Lederman, S. J. (1986). Tactual perception. In K. R. Boff, L. Kaufman, & J. P. Thomas (Eds) *Handbook of perception and human performance, vol. II* (chap. 31, pp. 1–41). New York: Wiley.

McBurney, D. H., & Shick, T. R. (1971). Taste and water taste of twenty-six compounds for man. *Perception and Psychophysics, 10*, 249–252.

McBurney, D. H., Collings, V. B., & Glanz, L. M. (1973). Temperature dependence of human taste responses. *Physiology and Behavior, 11*, 89–94.

McClintock, M. K. (1971). Menstrual synchrony and suppression. *Nature 229*, 244–245.

McClintock, M. K. (1984). Estrous synchrony: Modulation of ovarian cycle length by female pheromones. *Physiology and Behavior, 32*, 701–705.

Melzack, R. (1973). *The puzzle of pain*. New York: Basic Books.

Melzack, R., & Wall, P. D. (1965). Pain mechanisms: A new theory. *Science, 150*, 971–979.

Melzack, R., & Wall, P. D. (1982). *The challenge of pain*. New York: Basic Books.

Moncrieff, R. W. (1951). *The chemical senses*. London: Leonard Hill.

Morris, D. B. (1991). *The culture of pain*. Berkeley, CA: University of California Press.

Mozell, M. M. (1971). Olfaction. In J. W. Kling & L. A. Riggs (Eds) *Experimental psychology* (3rd edn) (pp. 193–222). New York: Holt, Rinehart & Winston.

Murphy, C. (1987). Olfactory psychophysics. In T. E. Finger & W. L. Silver (Eds) *Neurobiology of taste and smell* (pp. 251–273). New York: Wiley.

Porter, R. H., Cernoch, J. M., & McLaughlin, F. J. (1983). Maternal recognition of neonates through olfactory cues. *Physiology and Behavior, 30*, 151–154.

Porter, R. H., Balogh, R. D., Cernoch, J. M., & Franchi, C. (1986). Recognition of kin through characteristic body odors. *Chemical Senses, 11*, 389–395.

Preti, G., Cutler, W. B., Garcia, C. R., Huggins, G. R., & Lawley, H. J. (1986). Human axillary secretions influence women's menstrual cycles: The role of donor extract of females. *Hormones and Behavior, 20*, 474–482.

Quadagno, D. M., Shubeita, H. E., Deck, J., & Francoeur, D. (1981). Influence of male social contacts, exercise and all female living conditions on the menstrual cycle. *Psychoneuroendocrinology, 6*, 239–244.

Reed, C. M., Doherty, M. J., Braida, L. D., & Durlach, N. I. (1982). Analytic study of the Tadoma method: Further experiments with inexperienced observers. *Journal of Speech and Hearing Research, 25*, 216–223.

Russell, M. J. (1976). Human olfactory communication. *Nature, 260*, 520–522.

Russell, M. J., Switz, G. M., & Thompson, K. (1980). Olfactory influence on the human menstrual cycle. *Pharmacology, Biochemistry and Behavior, 13*, 737–738.

Schiffman, H. R. (1990). *Sensation and perception: An integrated approach* (3rd edn). New York: Wiley.

Schiffman, S. S. (1974). Physiochemical correlates of olfactory quality. *Science, 185*, 112–117.

Schiffman, S. S., Moss, J., & Erickson, R. P. (1976). Thresholds of food odors in the elderly. *Experimental Aging Research, 2*, 389–398.

Shepard, R. N. (1967). Recognition memory for words, sentences, and pictures. *Journal of Verbal Learning and Verbal Behavior, 6*, 156–163.

Terman, C. G., Shavit, Y., Lewis, J. W., Cannon, J. T., & Liebeskind, J. C. (1984). Intrinsic mechanisms of pain inhibition: Activation by stress. *Science, 226*, 1270–1277.

Vierling, J. S., & Rock, J. (1967). Variations of olfactory sensitivity to Exaltolide during the menstrual cycle. *Journal of Applied Physiology*, *22*, 311–315.

Wallace, P. (1977). Individual discrimination of humans by odor. *Physiology and Behavior*, *19*, 577–579.

Weinstein, S. (1968). Intensive and extensive aspects of tactile sensitivity as a function of body part, sex, and laterality. In D. R. Kenshalo (Ed.) *The skin senses* (chap. 10). Springfield, IL: Charles C. Thomas.

White, B. W., Saunders, F. A., Scadden, L., Bach-y-Rita, P., & Collins C. C. (1970). Seeing with the skin. *Perception and Psychophysics*, *7*, 23–27.

Young, L. R. (1984). Perception of the body in space: Mechanisms. In I. Darian-Smith (Ed.) *Handbook of physiology: The nervous system, III* (pp. 1023–1066). Bethesda, MD: American Physiological Society.

5

PSYCHOPHYSICS

Donald Laming
University of Cambridge, England

Psychophysics is really about the measurement of the strength of internal sensations and I emphasize that *sensation* is a technical term. It must not be confused with the physical magnitude of the stimulus. Three examples will make the distinction clear.

First, you wake up early on a dark winter's morning and put the bedroom light on to see the time. Initially you are dazzled; but after a few seconds your eyes adapt to the light which then seems much less bright. The (physical) luminance of the light is one thing, its apparent (subjective) brightness quite another.

Second, suppose, now, you are listening to TV late at night. Although the volume control has not been touched, the sound nevertheless appears gradually to get louder. If you listen past midnight, your next-door neighbour may well protest about a level of sound that passed unnoticed earlier in the evening. The loudness of the sound as you (and your neighbour) hear it is not the same as the auditory power produced by the TV set's loudspeaker.

Third, there is a trick question: which is heavier, a pound of feathers or a pound of lead? Without thinking, you say "lead" – and are then told that they both weigh the same! But if "heaviness" means the feel of weight as one or the other is picked up, the pound of lead is indeed heavier. Dense materials feel heavier, weight for weight, than materials of lesser density; this is known as the size-weight illusion. In my classroom demonstration a pillow weighing 720 gm is repeatedly judged to be equal to a lead weight somewhere between 30 and 225 gm. The feel of heaviness is distinct from the physical weight of the object.

In what follows I distinguish carefully between the physical measurement of a stimulus – luminance, sound pressure level, weight – and its subjective counterpart – brightness, loudness, heaviness. To emphasize this distinction I use two separate sets of words. Luminance, sound pressure level, and weight can be measured with photometers, sound level meters, and scale pans to whatever accuracy may be desired. But how can one measure internal quantities like brightness, loudness and heaviness? Such measurement is the subject of this chapter.

MEASUREMENTS OF THE DISCRIMINABILITY BETWEEN STIMULI

Suppose you lift a weight of 100 gm and then one of 200 gm; the second weight is obviously heavier. But suppose the second weight is 101 gm? Would the difference be obvious then? As the 100 gm weight is compared with progressively heavier second weights, there comes a point at which the difference is "just noticeable". In 1860 Fechner proposed using that "just noticeable difference" as a unit (like a foot or a pound) to measure internal sensation.

Fechner's idea works like this. Take the 100 gm weight and a selection of heavier weights to discover which of them is just noticeably greater. In an experiment the weights are usually made up by setting a requisite amount of lead shot in wax at the bottom of a tin can. Each weight is housed in an identical can so that there is no visual indication which weight is which. Suppose 105 gm is judged to be just noticeably greater than 100 gm. Now find the weight which is just noticeably greater than 105 gm, and then the weight just noticeably greater than that, and so on. A ladder of weights is constructed in which the step from one weight to the next is always "just noticeable". Fechner proposed using that ladder as a scale of internal sensation.

There are some practical problems of which the most pressing is how to measure "just noticeable differences". It happens that the minimum resolvable difference in weight (and in many other attributes as well) bears a simple relation to the standard weight with which comparison is being made. But the problem of ascertaining the constant ratio which enters into that relation remains. Fechner devoted nine years to experimental research exploring three different methods of measuring that constant ratio; eventually, in 1860, he published his *Elemente der Psychophysik*, a book which did more than any other single publication to make psychology an experimental science. In that book Fechner sketched out a "physics of the mind" which he called *psychophysics*. But the preliminary to any such exploration of mental function must be reliable measurement of internal sensations.

The method of constant stimuli

Suppose a subject lifts two weights, 100 gm and $100 + \Delta$ gm, where Δ is a small increase. After lifting the two weights the subject says which she thinks is greater. Figure 1 presents data from Brown (1910), for the comparison of

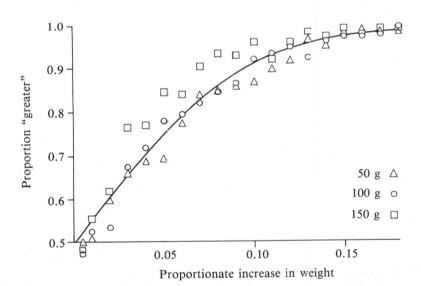

Figure 1 Discrimination of lifted weights by the method of constant stimuli. Each data point shows the proportion of correct judgements in 200 trials. The continuous curve is the upper half of a normal integral

Source: Data from Brown, 1910, Table II, pp. 16–17, Rows M, N, and O; figure from Laming, 1986, p. 22. Copyright Academic Press, 1986. Reproduced by permission

standard weights of 50, 100, and 150 gm with a range of percentage increases. The proportion of "greater" judgements increases smoothly throughout this range. This means that there is no precise increase in weight which can obviously be said to be "just noticeably different". Instead, a *just noticeable difference*, more frequently called a *difference threshold* or simply *threshold*, has to be defined as a statistical concept, most often that difference which is judged correctly 75 per cent of the time (though other percentages are sometimes used). The curve in Figure 1 is the upper half of a normal integral, the cumulative function of a normal distribution. When the subject is comparing two separate stimuli, this curve has repeatedly been found to provide a good representation of the way in which the proportion of correct judgements increases with the stimulus difference. This relation was first proposed by Fechner (1860).

The method of limits

In the method of limits there is a standard stimulus (100 gm) which is fixed and a comparison which is increased or decreased by small predetermined steps. The scheme is illustrated in Figure 2. Starting at a value clearly less

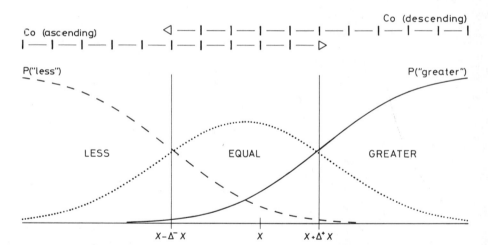

Figure 2 A diagram to illustrate the method of limits. A graduated series of increasing comparison stimuli are successively compared with a fixed standard (X) to determine the point at which "less" gives way to "equal" and the greater point at which "equal" gives way to "greater". Ascending series of comparisons are balanced by an equal number of descending series. The *upper difference threshold* Δ^+X is determined by that value which is judged greater than the standard 50 per cent of the time; likewise the *lower difference threshold* Δ^-X by the value judged "less than" 50 per cent of the time

Source: Laming, 1986, p. 19. Copyright Academic Press, 1986. Reproduced by permission

than the standard, the comparison stimulus is increased until the subject says "equal" and then increased further until she says "greater". The objective is to determine what value of the comparison stimulus would be judged less than the standard 50 per cent of the time (the difference $\Delta^- X$ with respect to the standard X in Figure 2 is known as the *lower difference threshold*) and what greater value of the comparison would be judged "greater than", again 50 per cent of the time (giving the *upper difference threshold* $\Delta^+ X$ in Figure 2). Ascending sequences of comparison values are balanced by descending sequences because subjects tend to perseverate their judgements. Ascending series usually give higher estimates of the 50 per cent values than do descending series.

Figure 3 shows a sample of measurements by this method from Kiesow (1925/1926). The stimuli were horizontal lines, about $\frac{1}{3}$ mm thick, drawn in black ink on white paper. The length of the comparison line was varied by covering part of it with another sheet of paper. The open triangles are upper thresholds determined from ascending series of comparison stimuli, and the

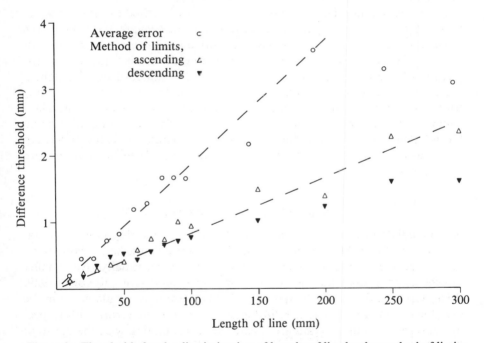

Figure 3 Thresholds for the discrimination of lengths of line by the method of limits and the method of average error. The thresholds by the method of average error (circles) are plotted against the mean adjustment as abscissa, rather than the standard stimulus

Source: The data, all from the same subject, are from Kiesow, 1925/1926; the figure is from Laming, 1986, p. 20. Copyright Academic Press, 1986. Reproduced by permission

filled triangles are from descending series. Most of the estimates from ascending series are greater than the corresponding estimates from descending series.

The method of average error

The circles in Figure 3 are thresholds obtained from the same subject for the same lines drawn on paper, but using the third of Fechner's methods, the method of average error. In this procedure the subject's task is simply to adjust the length of one line (by moving the sheet of paper which partially overlays it) so that it matches the length of another line (the standard). There is some restriction of the subject's opportunity to compare the two lines; they are placed end to end, not side by side. The adjustment of the comparison line to match the standard is, of course, different each time, and several matches are made to each standard length. The threshold is usually taken to be the probable error of adjustment, that is, the absolute error which would be exceeded in 50 per cent of such matches.

The same standard lengths were used as with the method of limits (and are represented in Figure 3 by the abscissa values of the *triangles*); the data from the method of average error (circles) are plotted against *mean adjustment* as abscissa. This manner of presentation shows that the mean adjustment in the method of average error was always less than the standard to be matched; the abscissa values of the circles lie always to the left of the corresponding triangles. It is common for the mean adjustment to deviate from the standard stimulus; the difference is known as the *constant error* to distinguish it from the *variable error* which is different for each separate matching. Constant errors also appear in the other two methods, but are most obvious with average error.

Comparison of the three methods

An immediate problem for Fechner's scheme for measuring internal sensations is that these three methods typically do not give the same value for a just noticeable difference. The method of average error usually gives smaller thresholds than does the method of constant stimuli (e.g., Kellogg, 1929; Wier, Jesteadt, & Green, 1976) provided the threshold is calculated from the variable errors alone. (The data in Figure 3 are absolute errors with respect to the standard stimulus and are inflated by confounding with the constant error.) A possible explanation was suggested by Stephanowitsch (1913) who recorded all the separate comparisons made by subjects while adjusting the length of one line to match another. There were many more comparisons of small differences than of large; this biases the ultimate estimate of the threshold.

Comparisons with the method of limits are uncertain. This method realizes more directly than the other two the nineteenth-century conception of a "threshold" as a limit below which nothing can be perceived — like the threshold in a doorway. That idea is now known to be misconceived (see Laming, 1986, chap. 3; Swets, Tanner, & Birdsall, 1961) and the method has accordingly fallen into disuse. Contemporary practice is based on the picture presented in Figure 1 in which the probability of a correct judgement increases smoothly as the stimulus difference increases. Modern methods aim to estimate some chosen point on this function (often, but not always, the 75 per cent point) with as few trials as possible. This is accomplished by adjusting the comparison stimulus from one trial to the next, up or down, according to the subject's responses. A variety of schemes, sometimes known as *staircase procedures*, have been devised by Cornsweet (1962), Levitt (1971), and others. The ultimate in the efficient use of experimental trials is QUEST (Watson & Pelli, 1983; see also Laming & Marsh, 1988). QUEST achieves its efficiency by utilizing certain prior knowledge about the function in Figure 1.

Weber's Law

Notwithstanding the difficulties in measuring thresholds, one important generalization can be made. In Figure 1 the same percentage increase with respect to standards of 50, 100, 150 gm gives nearly the same proportion of correct responses. This means that the difference threshold increases in proportion to the standard. The same relation is evident in the data from the method of limits in Figure 3.

Let ΔW be the 75 per cent threshold measured at a standard weight W. (ΔW means a small, but not vanishingly small, increment in weight.) Then

$$\Delta W / W = \text{constant.} \tag{1}$$

This is known as *Weber's Law* after E. H. Weber who first enunciated it in 1834. It holds approximately for many stimulus attributes down to about the absolute threshold which is the smallest magnitude of stimulus that can be perceived (see Laming, 1986, pp. 76–77, Table 5.1).

Fechner's Law

Fechner proposed measuring internal sensations in units of "just noticeable differences". Suppose that sensation S increases as the logarithm of the physical stimulus magnitude. If weights are being lifted,

$$S = \log W. \tag{2}$$

If ΔS is the just noticeable increase in heaviness produced by the increase in ΔW in weight,

$$S + \Delta S = \log(W + \Delta W). \tag{3}$$

Subtracting Equation 2 from Equation 3 gives, for the just noticeable increase in sensation,

$$\Delta S = \log(W + \Delta W) - \log W$$
$$= \log(1 + \Delta W/W), \tag{4}$$

because the difference of two logarithms is equal to the logarithm of their ratio.

If, in Equation 4, ΔS is constant, so also is $\Delta W/W$, which is Weber's Law (Equation 1). This means that, if Weber's Law applies to the stimulus attribute in question and just noticeable differences in sensation are taken to be equal, then sensation increases as the logarithm of the physical stimulus magnitude. Equation 2 is known as *Fechner's Law*. I have argued here from Fechner's Law to Weber's Law. Fechner (1860) had to argue in the opposite direction, which is more difficult (see Krantz, 1971; Luce & Edwards, 1958).

"DIRECT" MEASUREMENTS OF SENSATION

Fechner's Law was long accepted as the relation between internal sensation and physical stimulus magnitude, chiefly because there was no serious alternative. But about the year 1930 a practical problem arose in acoustic engineering. The sounds that we ordinarily hear vary over a very wide range, so wide that sound level is conventionally measured in decibels on a logarithmic scale. The quietest sound that can just be heard is rated 0 dB and each tenfold increase in power above that level adds 10 dB to the rating. Table 1 lists some common environmental sounds against their approximate decibel values.

Because the decibel rating increases as the logarithm of the physical power of the sound, it ought to be proportional to the sensation produced. But most people would say that 100 dB (an underground train coming into a station) sounds much more than twice as loud as 50 dB (the background noise of conversation in a library). When acoustic engineers have to explain to their clients how loud things are going to sound, the false impression given by the decibel scale matters.

There were some experiments conducted by acoustic engineers in the early 1930s. A typical trial presented two tones and asked: how many times louder was the second tone than the first? Alternatively the subject might adjust the second tone to be twice or half as loud as the first. The results of those experiments were assembled by S. S. Stevens (1936) into the *sone* scale of loudness. Taking a 1,000 Hz (cycles per second) tone as the standard sound, a tone at

Table 1   Decibel levels of some common environmental sounds

Sound	Sound level in dB
Softest audible sound	0
Normal breathing	10
Open country at night	20
Soft whisper	30
Very quiet living room	40
Quiet conversation (e.g., library)	50
Average speaking voice at 5 ft	60
Television, typical sound level	70
Motor car at 65 mph, from 25 ft	80
Motor cycle 25 ft away	90
Underground train entering station	100
Chain saw (unprotected operator)	110
Loud rock group	120
Machine-gun fire at close range	130
Jet engine at take-off, from 100 ft	140

40 dB was defined to have a loudness of 1 sone, at 50 dB 2 sones, at 60 dB 4 sones, at 70 dB 8 sones, and so on, the number of sones doubling with each increase of 10 dB. The loudnesses of other sounds were then measured by matching to a 1,000 Hz tone.

The difference with respect to the decibel scale is worth emphasis. If the intensity (physical power) of a sound is increased tenfold, its dB rating increases always by 10, but its sone rating is doubled. The fixed dB increase for a constant multiplicative increase in intensity makes the dB scale logarithmic, like Fechner's scale of sensation. But the doubling of the sone rating means that it increases as a (mathematical) power of intensity. Put into an equation

$$\text{Loudness in sones} = (10^{-2} A/A_0)^{0.6} \tag{5}$$

where A is the amplitude of the physical sound wave and A_0 is the faintest amplitude that can be heard (0 dB). The sone scale (Equation 5) constituted the first serious alternative to Fechner's Law (Equation 2).

Magnitude estimation

Twenty years later S. S. Stevens (1956, 1957) returned to the problem of measuring sensation and developed his method of *magnitude estimation*. Figure 4 displays the results from an experiment which Stevens (1975) presented as typical.

In this experiment the stimuli, eight 1,000 Hz tones ranging from 40 to 110 dB, were presented one at a time in random order. They were presented

105

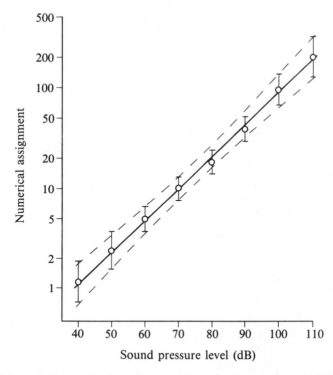

Figure 4 Numerical magnitude estimates of the loudness of a 1000 Hz tone by 32 observers judging each stimulus twice only. The vertical bar through each data point shows the inter-quartile range of the 64 judgements. The broken curves are predictions for the inter-quartile ranges

Source: Adapted and redrawn from S. S. Stevens, 1975, p. 28

twice each to 32 subjects, in a different random order to each subject. The first tone heard was given any number considered appropriate; thereafter, the instruction was "Try to make the ratios between the numbers you assign to the different tones correspond to the ratios between the loudnesses of the tones" (S. S. Stevens, 1956, p. 20). There was no suggestion that there was such a thing as a "correct" response; "We are interested in how loud tones *seem* to be to you, not in some kind of 'accuracy'." (S. S. Stevens, 1956, p. 17). The intention was to record the subject's internal experiences as simply and directly as possible.

Some subjects tended to use larger numbers than others; the numbers in Figure 4 have been scaled so that the geometric mean of each subject's scaled judgements is the same. After scaling, the mean judgements accord closely with the sone scale (Equation 5 above; Figure 4 has been plotted with logarithmic ordinate and abscissa: this way of presenting the data turns the power relation of Equation 5 into a straight line of gradient equal to the exponent). The vertical bars in Figure 4 mark the inter-quartile intervals of the magnitude estimates and the broken curve describes predictions for those intervals. The intervals and their predictions will be discussed later.

Stevens' Power Law

Magnitude estimation was developed by S. S. Stevens (1956) as an experimental procedure after much trial and error. While some psychologists have reported difficulty in replicating the experiment, in the hands of Stevens and his colleagues it has given nicely repeatable results. It has been applied to a very large number of different stimulus attributes; S. S. Stevens (1975, p. 15) lists 33. The results from each attribute conform approximately to an equation of the form

$$\text{Mean magnitude estimate} = aX^b \qquad (6)$$

where X is the physical measurement of the stimulus, a a scale factor, and b an exponent characteristic of the attribute. That exponent (b) has been found to vary from 0.33 (brightness) to 3.5 (electric shock). The exponent for length, of which most people have much experience, is approximately 1.0. Equation 6 is known as *Stevens' Power Law*.

Magnitude production

If subjects can systematically assign numbers to stimuli, can they also adjust stimuli to match given numbers? Figure 5 presents an example from S. S. Stevens and Greenbaum (1966).

The stimulus in this experiment was an interval of time marked by a burst of white noise. In the first phase of the experiment ten subjects made two separate judgements each of the durations of twelve different bursts of white noise. Their geometric mean estimates are shown by the open circles in Figure 5 and the standard deviations of these estimates by the lengths of the broken lines. In the second phase of the experiment the same subjects pressed a key to produce a noise burst of appropriate duration in response to each of eight different numbers. Those numbers were chosen in the light of the mean responses in the first phase. The geometric mean productions are shown by the filled circles in Figure 5 and their respective standard deviations (it is now the abscissa value which is set by the subjects) by the continuous straight lines. Both sets of means are approximately linear on this log-log plot in accord with Stevens' Power Law. But the gradients of the two lines (and therefore the values of the exponent in the power law) differ. The mean productions (filled circles) are steeper (higher exponent) than the estimates (open circles).

This difference in gradient, depending on whether magnitudes are being estimated or produced, is usually small, but is, at the same time, highly

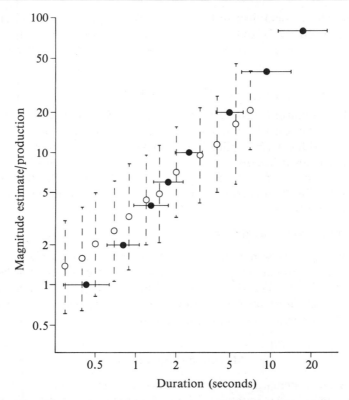

Figure 5 Matching of numbers to the durations of bursts of noise. The open circles are geometric mean magnitude estimates and the filled circles magnitude productions. The vertical and horizontal lines through the data points extend to ±1 standard deviation of the distribution of logarithm matches
Source: Data from S. S. Stevens and Greenbaum, 1966, Table 2, p. 444

systematic. The difference always lies in the direction illustrated in Figure 5, with productions giving a steeper gradient than estimates, and may be succinctly summarized by the dictum "The observer tends to shorten the range of which ever variable he controls" (S. S. Stevens, 1971, p. 426). Stevens and Greenbaum (1966) called this the "regression effect".

Cross-modality matching

If subjects can assign numbers to stimuli and adjust stimuli to match numbers, presumably they can also adjust one stimulus to match another, the stimuli being of quite different kinds. J. C. Stevens, J. D. Mack, and S. S. Stevens (1960) had subjects match values of a number of different attributes to force of handgrip. The subjects squeezed a hand dynamometer to whatever extent seemed to match the intensity of electric current, or white noise, or vibration, or whatever, presented for matching. Figure 6 shows their results.

Other experiments have determined exponent values for numerical estimation of all the attributes represented in Figure 5. Suppose, for example, that the assignment of numbers to a 1,000 Hz tone accords with the equation

$$N = X^b \tag{7}$$

and the assignment to force of handgrip to

$$M = Y^c. \tag{8}$$

If Stevens' Power Law derives from some real transformation of the neural message inside the sensory system, as Stevens (1970) believed, the matching of force of handgrip directly to the loudness of a 1,000 Hz tone should be predictable from Equations 7 and 8. Briefly, when a value of Y is matched to a value of X, the number (N) assigned by Equation 7 should equate to the other number (M) assigned by Equation 8; that is, the force of handgrip

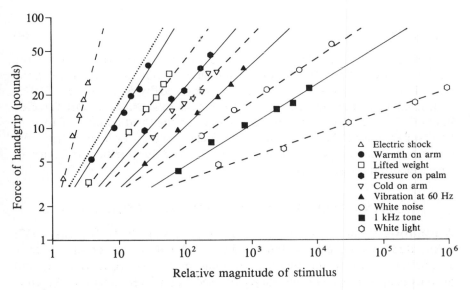

Figure 6 Force of handgrip matched to values of ten other stimulus attributes. Each set of data has been arbitrarily transposed along the abscissa for clarity of presentation. The dotted line represents a gradient of 1
Source: Redrawn from S. S. Stevens, 1966, p 5

Table 2 Calculation of predicted exponents in Figure 6

Stimulus attribute	Numerical estimates (b)	Predicted exponent	Matching by force of handgrip (b|c)
Electric shock	3.5	2.06	2.13
Force of handgrip	1.7(c)	—	—
Warmth on arm	1.6	0.94	0.96
Lifted weight	1.45	0.85	0.79
Pressure on palm	1.1	0.65	0.67
Cold on arm	1.0	0.59	0.60
Vibration at 60 Hz	0.95	0.56	0.56
White noise	0.67	0.39	0.41
1,000 Hz tone	0.67	0.39	0.35
White light	0.33	0.19	0.21

(Y) matched to the sound level (X) should satisfy

$$Y^c = X^b$$

or

$$Y = X^{b/c}. \tag{9}$$

Table 2 sets out calculations which show that this relation holds for the data in Figure 6. The estimates of the magnitude estimation exponents in the second column are taken from the list assembled by S. S. Stevens (1975, p. 15). Dividing each by the exponent for numerical estimation of force of handgrip (row 2, c) gives the predicted value in the third column. This is to be compared with the exponent in the fourth column estimated from the direct matching of force of handgrip with the stimulus attribute in Figure 6. The concordance is very good.

RELATING STEVENS' POWER LAW TO FECHNER'S LAW

A controversy has continued, on and off, ever since S. S. Stevens (1957) enunciated his law. Fechner (1860) had asserted that internal sensations grew as the logarithm of the physical stimulus magnitude (Equation 2), and Stevens proposed instead that they increased as a power function. Which is correct?

First, in principle, it is possible for both to be correct. A more general form of Fechner's Law (Equation 2) would be

$$S = \log a + b \log X \tag{10}$$

writing X for the physical magnitude of some arbitrary stimulus attribute.

Taking antilogarithms on both sides of Equation 10 gives

$$10^S = aX^b, \tag{11}$$

which is Stevens' Power Law (Equation 6) with "10^S" for "Mean magnitude estimate"; taking logarithms on both sides of Equation 6, of course, gives Fechner's Law (Equation 10). So it is possible that the controversy concerns no more than the way in which the mathematics should be formulated – whether the label "sensation" should be attached to magnitude estimates or to their logarithms.

Second, on the other hand, it could be that the logarithmic law and the power function are both wrong. Fechner and Stevens have attached the label "sensation" to different experimental measurements solely by fiat. Some extraneous justification is needed for taking either just noticeable differences or magnitude estimates as the measurement of internal sensation.

Such justification can come only from the role that each plays in some ultimate theory of sensory discrimination or of sensory judgement. It is the task of the natural scientist to describe the state of nature as accurately and succinctly as possible. If in such a theory of sensory discrimination there emerged a fundamental role for some function of the stimulus attribute distinct from the physical measurement (the logarithm, for example), that function might reasonably be taken to measure internal sensation. Likewise, if it were shown that magnitude estimates fulfilled such a role, the label "sensation" might reasonably be attached there. But this matter should not be decided without a careful examination of the results obtained from the different experiments.

In the rest of this chapter I show, first, that Fechner's Law and Stevens' Power Law cannot both be correct. The possible reconciliation sketched above is incompatible with existing experimental results. In fact, sensory discrimination and magnitude estimation study quite distinct psychological processes. Second, the findings about sensory discrimination, especially Weber's Law, which led to Fechner's logarithmic law, can be described more succinctly and comprehensively directly in terms of the physical measurement of the stimulus. Third, Stevens' results from magnitude estimation also admit a more comprehensive description in which the power law results from the way in which the experiment is set up and has no theoretical significance at all.

Reconciling Fechner's and Stevens' laws

If the controversy is solely about the way in which the mathematics should be formulated, then, whichever way that question is ultimately resolved, values on one attribute (X) should map on to values on some other attribute

(Y) according to Equation 9 (Stevens' Power Law), which I rewrite here in the form

$$Y^c = X^b. \tag{12}$$

At the same time, Fechner's Law requires a just noticeable increase in X to equate to an equally noticeable increase in Y. So

$$(Y + \Delta Y)^c = (X + \Delta X)^b. \tag{13}$$

Dividing Equation 13 by Equation 12 leads to

$$(1 + \Delta Y/Y)^c = (1 + \Delta X/X)^b \tag{14}$$

which relates the exponents from magnitude estimation (b, c) to the Weber fractions ($\Delta X/X$, $\Delta Y/Y$) from discrimination experiments. More to the point, the quantities on the left hand side of Equation 14 relate *solely* to attribute Y and those on the right *solely* to attribute X, whatever those attributes might be. It follows that

$$(1 + \Delta X/X)^b = \text{constant} \tag{15}$$

a constant that is independent of the stimulus attribute.

Equation 15 relates the Weber fraction to the magnitude estimation exponent. It was first derived by Teghtsoonian (1971) who tabulated data from nine different attributes. Teghtsoonian's calculated values for the constant range from 0.026 to 0.034, a closer concordance than one might expect in view of the difficulties of pairing different experiments by different experimenters using different apparatus in different laboratories. Careful examination of Teghtsoonian's sources shows that this concordance is, indeed, too good to be true (see Laming, 1989, p. 280).

Figure 7 presents my own collection of some 30 pairs of experimental values. The continuous line, not quite straight, is Equation 15 with the constant set equal to 0.052. The triangles are the particular attributes tabulated by Teghtsoonian (1971), but not necessarily estimated from the same data. Some of those attributes are here represented more than once. The filled symbols are pairings of Weber fractions and exponents from the *same experimenter*, usually from different experiments employing the same apparatus and published together. One might expect these pairings to be more precisely related than the open symbols which are based on two independent sources. But the scatter of the filled symbols is as great as that of the open ones. All that can be said of the predicted relation is that there are no attributes with both a small Weber fraction and a low exponent. Otherwise, there is no relation between the two.

112

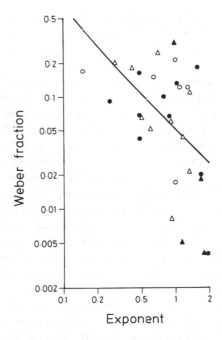

Figure 7 Weber fractions and power law exponents from some 30 pairs of experiments. The filled symbols are those pairs where both quantities have been estimated from the work of the same experimenter; open symbols are pairings of results from different experimenters. The triangles represent those attributes surveyed by Teghtsoonian (1971). The continuous line is Equation 15 with the constant set equal to 0.052

Source: Laming, 1989, p. 280. Copyright 1989 by Cambridge University Press. Reproduced by permission

Variability of magnitude estimates

If sensory discrimination and magnitude estimation were telling us about the *same* underlying psychological process, the precision of the two kinds of judgement should be about the same. The data in Figures 4 and 5 enable two comparisons.

First, the inter-quartile range of log. magnitude estimates in Figure 4 is at a minimum at 80 dB where it is ± 0.115 log. units. Individual estimates have been rescaled to eliminate differences of scale in the size of the numbers uttered by different subjects, so this inter-quartile interval relates entirely to intra-subject variation. For comparison with other experiments, it is convenient to convert this interval into an equivalent on the stimulus scale. Since log. loudness varies 0.6 in proportion to differences in log. amplitude (Equation 5), the equivalent interval on the stimulus scale is 0.19 log. units ($= 0.115/0.6$), which equates to a proportional 0.55 increase in amplitude. A

113

discrimination experiment with comparable stimuli has been reported by Jesteadt, Wier, and Green (1977). They found the Weber fraction for a 1,000 Hz tone at 80 dB to be 0.06 in amplitude units, less by a whole order of magnitude.

Second, the data in Figure 5 (open circles and broken lines) are magnitude estimates and standard deviations for intervals of time marked by bursts of white noise. The standard deviations range from 0.34 to 0.45 log. units (except for the longest duration, which has standard deviation 0.29). The power law exponent estimated from the means is 0.87, so that a standard deviation in log. magnitude estimate of 0.34 is equivalent to 0.39 log. units ($= 0.34/0.87$) with respect to log. time, that is, an increase of 1.46 or a decrease of 0.59. Discrimination of similar intervals of time has been studied by Treisman (1963) who found the corresponding standard deviation (that is, the threshold according to a criterion of 84 per cent correct) to vary between 0.066 and 0.174 in different experiments. Again, the variability of the magnitude estimates is greater by an order of magnitude.

The two experiments in each comparison employed substantially the same stimuli, so the initial sensory processing must be common. Since magnitude estimates are so much more variable than simple discriminations of "louder" or "softer", the magnitude estimation task must engage some further psychological process which contributes additional variance. The process studied by simple threshold experiments is *sensory discrimination*, and I call the additional process engaged by magnitude estimation *sensory judgement* (Laming, 1991). The standard deviation of magnitude estimates is typically ten times that of threshold discriminations in linear measure. But since variances add in square measure, the real contribution of variance from sensory judgement must be 100 times that from sensory discrimination. The two kinds of experiments, looking respectively at resolving power and at "direct" estimates of magnitude, cannot be studying the same process.

SENSORY DISCRIMINATION

The possibility of justifying one or the other measurement of sensation now depends on there being some fundamental role in sensory discrimination for Fechner's Law or in sensory judgement for Stevens' Power Law. Sensory discrimination lies beyond the scope of this chapter. But recent developments permit the question of the validity of Fechner's Law to be resolved.

A discrimination between two separate stimuli, any two values of an attribute conforming to Weber's Law, may be modelled very accurately by combining Fechner's Law with the normal distribution. Torgerson (1958, chap. 10) has set out the general idea; Thurstone's (1927) "Law of Comparative Judgement" and Tanner and Swets' (1954) signal-detection theory are particular instances of it. This looks at first sight to be the required justification for Fechner's Law; but, unfortunately, the model is not unique. Another model, equally accurate, can be constructed by combining the natural physical measurement of the stimulus, in similar manner, with a χ^2 distribution (Laming, 1986, pp. 71–78). This undermines whatever validity there might have been for Fechner's Law.

The choice between the two models is not, in fact, arbitrary. The first (normal) model works well for discriminations between two separate stimuli. It happens so because, under a logarithmic transform, the χ^2 model transforms into a very close approximation of the normal model (Laming, 1986, pp. 242–254) and, mathematically speaking, this is the reason why Fechner's Law takes the form that it does. But many sensory experiments add a brief increment to an existing stimulus background. The normal model cannot accommodate this different configuration of the stimulus levels to be distinguished, whereas the second (χ^2) model generalizes naturally to a more comprehensive model which takes in the detection of increments as well (Laming, 1986). For this reason the χ^2 model is to be preferred. There is no need, so far as sensory discrimination is concerned, to invoke any fundamental variable distinct from the physical measurement of the stimulus. Fechner's Law does not provide any basis for measuring internal sensations.

NUMERICAL ESTIMATION OF SENSORY MAGNITUDES

Fechner's Law fails to provide a basis for measuring sensation because the experimental phenomena on which it is based admit an alternative, and more comprehensive, account in terms of the physical measurement of the stimulus magnitude. Can the same be accomplished for magnitude estimation and the related procedures on which Stevens' Power Law is based? Note that the consistency check provided by cross-modality matching experiments is not itself sufficient to establish the validity of Stevens' Law. It is merely a constraint which any, and every, explanation has to satisfy.

Explanation of Stevens' Power Law

It is usual practice in magnitude estimation experiments to choose a geometric ladder of stimulus values so that each value is a fixed multiple of the one below it. Since the stimulus attributes commonly employed are those which conform to Weber's Law, this practice ensures that the discriminability of each stimulus from its neighbours is uniform throughout the scale. On a scale of log. stimulus magnitude the values are equally spaced.

It is also common for subjects to use *round* numbers in judging sensory magnitudes: 1, 2, 5, 10, 20, 50, 100, and so on (cf. Baird, Lewis, & Romer, 1975). This means that the numerical responses are also spread, more or less uniformly, on an approximately logarithmic scale. This practice is enhanced by instructing the subjects to judge ratios, as Stevens typically did (S. S. Stevens, 1971, p. 428). All that is now needed to complete a model for magnitude estimation is some scheme for a partially random assignment of numbers to stimulus values. The mapping of numbers on to stimuli is then estimated by regressing *log. number* on to *log. stimulus magnitude*, that is, by using an equation like

$$\log N = \log a + b \log X. \tag{16}$$

When antilogs are taken on both sides of Equation 13, it turns into Equation 6.

When the exponent b is estimated in this manner, its value will be approximately equal to the difference between the largest and smallest of the log. mean numerical estimates (i.e, the range of $\log N$) divided by the difference between the largest and smallest log. stimulus magnitudes (i.e., the range of $\log X$). That suggests looking at the relations between the estimates of the exponents for different stimulus attributes and the ranges of $\log N$ and $\log X$ in the corresponding experiments.

The relation between the exponent and log. stimulus range is plotted in Figure 8. The data points cluster closely around the hyperbola

$$b = 1.48/(\text{Log. Stimulus Range}). \tag{17}$$

This relation was discovered by Poulton (1967), but put into this striking form by Teghtsoonian (1971). If all the points lay exactly on the hyperbola,

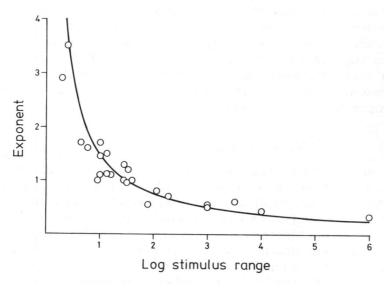

Figure 8 Power law exponents for 24 stimulus attributes plotted against the logarithm of the geometric range of stimulus values employed in the experiments from which the exponents were estimated. The continuous curve is the hyperbola of Equation 17
Source: After Teghtsoonian, 1971, p. 73

Stevens' laboratory was always the same, and that the exponent varied from one stimulus attribute to another solely because the range of stimulus values was different. That is not quite the picture in Figure 8, but very nearly.

The smallest stimulus range in Figure 8 is 2 (for the saturation of yellow) and the largest 1,000,000 (for brightness). So the stimulus ranges vary over 5.7 log. units. The smallest response range is 7.4 (again for saturation of yellow) and the largest is 138.33 (for binaural sound intensity). So the response ranges vary only over 1.27 log. units. It is not quite true to say that the response range is independent of the stimulus range, but the relationship is no more than slight.

Figure 8 suggests that Stevens' experimental results are most succinctly viewed as the mapping of a nearly constant logarithmic range of numbers on to a chosen logarithmic range of stimulus values. The stimulus range is usually chosen to be the largest practicable because this affords the most accurate estimate of the exponent. That largest practicable stimulus range depends on the attribute being studied, and the relation between exponent and stimulus attribute is generated thereby.

Relativity of judgement

If magnitude estimation is a mapping, subject to considerable variability, of a logarithmic range of numbers on to a logarithmic range of stimuli, it needs to be explained how this is accomplished.

Laming (1984) proposed this Principle of Relativity:

All judgements are relative to the immediate context.

In a magnitude estimation experiment the immediate context is the stimulus presented on the preceding trial and the number assigned to it. Judgement of the present stimulus relative to that context is no more than ordinal. This is implicit in the Principle of Relativity for this reason:

Suppose one stimulus is judged to be twice the magnitude of its predecessor. If that predecessor has itself been judged to be three times *its* predecessor, then the present stimulus is six times the stimulus presented two trials ago. Working backwards in this manner, all stimuli can be related to the standard presented at the beginning of the experiment. It is implicit in the Principle of Relativity that such backwards reference is impossible and judgements no better than ordinal.

Suppose, instead, each stimulus to be judged "greater than" or "about equal to" or "less than" its predecessor. If a stimulus is judged "greater than" the one before it, it is given a greater number; if "equal", the same number; if "less than", a smaller number. The question now is how will the numbers fall over a long run of judgements of randomly chosen stimulus values?

117

Small stimuli will usually be judged smaller than their respective predecessors and be assigned smaller numbers. For the complementary reason large stimuli will be assigned larger numbers. If the stimulus values are chosen in geometric progression, spaced equally on a logarithmic scale, and if the subjects are induced to use round numbers, to judge ratios — both these features were frequent in experiments by S. S. Stevens and his colleagues — it is appropriate to think in terms of logarithmic stimulus and response scales. The explanation of Stevens' Power Law above is thereby concordant with the Principle of Relativity, and in what follows I am concerned only with the variability of magnitude estimates. Laming (1984) expressed the consequences of the assumption of purely ordinal judgement in a quantitative model. In the interests of simplicity, I present here only a verbal characterization of that model and two of its predictions.

The estimation of the loudness in Figure 4 used a set of eight 1,000 Hz tones spaced at 10 dB intervals. The softest tone (40 dB) was preceded equally, on different trials, by each of the other seven and that variation in the point of reference increased the variability of the responses to the 40 dB tone. The variance of any one estimate includes a component which increases as the *square* of the (logarithmic) distance of the stimulus being judged from its predecessor. Since the 40 dB tone is more remote from 110 dB than, say, 70 or 80 dB is from either end of the scale, so the overall variability of the judgements is greater for the extreme stimuli (40 and 110 dB) than it is for the central ones. The broken curves in Figure 4 are numerical predictions derived by Laming (1984) for this particular experiment.

Autocorrelation of successive judgements

Figure 9 presents certain statistics from a magnitude estimation experiment by Baird, Green, and Luce (1980). The stimuli in this experiment were again 1,000 Hz tones ranging from 40 to 90 dB in steps of 2.5 dB. There were three subjects who made about 2,500 judgements each, randomly distributed over these 21 different stimuli. The statistics in Figure 9 are *autocorrelations* between successive log. numerical estimates in relation to the difference in dB between the corresponding stimulus values.

To explain the notion of correlation: suppose two examiners are each marking the same set of scripts. Examiner X assigns marks x_1, x_2, x_3, and so on, and Examiner Y marks y_1, y_2, y_3, ... to Scripts 1, 2, 3, ... Ideally, one would like these two examiners, each assigning marks independently of the other, to agree closely, because then one would have confidence in their marking. The correlation coefficient measures the closeness of their agreement.

Denote the average of Examiner X's marks by $\bar{x}$. Then $(x_1 - \bar{x})$ is the deviation of the mark assigned to Script 1 from that mean, and the average of terms like $(x_1 - \bar{x})^2$ is the variance of Examiner X's marks. If there are n

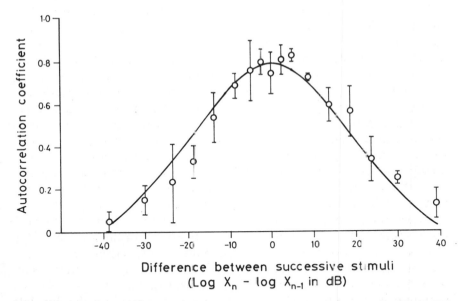

Figure 9 Coefficients of correlation between the logarithms of successive numerical estimates of loudness in relation to the dB difference between the tones. The circles show the mean coefficient from three subjects and the vertical bars extend to ±1 standard deviation. The quadratic curve is the prediction derived by Laming (1984, pp. 168–70)

Source: Adapted and redrawn from Baird, Green, and Luce, 1980, p. 286

scripts in the set to be marked, the variance is most accurately estimated by

$$\Sigma_i \, (x_i - \bar{x})^2/(n - 1) \tag{18}$$

where $i = 1, 2, 3, \ldots$ indexes the different scripts. Similar expressions can be calculated from Examiner Y's marks; one can also calculate the sum of cross-products like $(x_1 - \bar{x})(y_1 - \bar{y})$. Suppose the two examiners averages are the same. If they also assign the same mark to Script 1, the cross-product will equal $(x_1 - \bar{x})^2$; if they assign the same mark to every script (i.e., they agree perfectly), the average cross-product (dividing by $n - 1$) will equal the variance of each examiner's marks. It is therefore conventional to measure the correlation as the average of the cross-products divided by the geometric average of the variances (which are usually not the same). This leads to the expression

$$\text{Correlation coefficient} = \frac{\Sigma_i (x_i - \bar{x})(y_i - \bar{y})}{\sqrt{[\{\Sigma_i(x_i - \bar{x})^2\}\{\Sigma_i(x_i - \bar{x})^2\}]}} \tag{19}$$

which necessarily lies between +1 (perfect agreement) and −1 (complete disagreement).

In a magnitude estimation experiment there is only a *single* series of numerical judgements, N_i, where i indexes the ordinal number of the trial. Substitute $\log N_i$ for x_i in Formula 19 and $\log N_{i+1}$ for y_i. Each log. numerical judgement is then compared with its successor in the series: this is called *autocorrelation*. It is sensitive to any interdependence between successive judgements and might be indicative of the underlying process by which they are produced. In Figure 9 the pairs of successive judgements are sorted according to the decibel difference between the corresponding stimuli. When there is a large change in the level of the tone, there is little correlation between successive judgements; but when the level varies by no more than ± 5 dB from one stimulus to the next, the logarithms of the successive numbers are correlated about $+0.8$. That is to say, locally high values of $\log N_i$ generate high values of $\log N_{i+1}$ on the following trial, and this comes about because the number uttered on trial i is used as a point of reference for the judgement on trial $i+1$. In fact, $0.64\,(=0.8^2)$ of the variance of $\log N_{i+1}$ is inherited from $\log N_i$. On this basis Laming (1984) was able to calculate the quadratic curve in Figure 9 as a model for the correlation coefficients obtained in the experiment. This autocorrelation of successive log. magnitude estimates is the most compelling evidence of all for the Principle of Relativity, that each judgement uses its predecessor as a point of reference.

CONCLUSIONS

To complete this chapter I summarize the conclusions that may be drawn about the various experiments purporting to measure internal sensations and spell out what those conclusions mean for the notion of sensation.

First, there is an essential distinction to be drawn between the physical luminance, power, or weight of the stimulus and the brightness, loudness, and heaviness which one experiences.

Second, Fechner (1860) sought to measure internal sensation in terms of ability to distinguish one stimulus from another. Although the logarithmic transform implicit in Fechner's Law affords a simple and accurate account of a wide range of experimental results concerning the discrimination of one stimulus from another, an equally simple and accurate account may be had from a model based directly on the physical stimulus magnitude (Laming, 1986). Moreover, that equally simple and accurate account generalizes, in a way that the logarithmic model does not, to accommodate a significantly wider range of experimental findings, taking in the detection of increments to an existing stimulus background. There is, therefore, no justification in the study of sensory discrimination for taking Fechner's Law as descriptive of internal sensation.

Third, as an alternative, S. S. Stevens (1957) proposed a power law relation between physical stimulus magnitude and internal sensation. That relation concisely summarized the averaged results of many experiments using

120

magnitude estimation and related procedures by S. S. Stevens and his colleagues. Comparison of the variance of magnitude estimates with the corresponding precision of discrimination in experiments using substantially the same stimuli shows that magnitude estimation studies a different and much more variable process (which I have called *sensory judgement*) than sensory discrimination.

Fourth, as before, a more comprehensive account of S. S. Stevens' results, including, especially, the variability of magnitude estimates, is afforded by the idea that judgements of sensation are no more than ordinal. According to this account, Stevens' Power Law is a by-product of the way that the experiments have been designed and conducted and the value of the power law exponent, different for different stimulus attributes, is determined chiefly by the geometric range of stimulus values used.

The nature of sensation

Finally, existing experiments do not support any measurement of internal sensation analogous to the measurement of length and weight. The most that subjects can validly say is that this light is brighter than that one, this sound louder than that, this weight heavier than that. Fechner's original conception of a "physics of the mind" is not realizable. On the other hand, the experiments by S. S. Stevens and many others addressing this question have provided a wealth of data on how numerical judgements are formulated. Once those data are disentangled from traditional misunderstandings about internal sensation, the way is open for the study of the wide range of mental phenomena subsumed in sensory judgement, a study which is only just beginning.

FURTHER READING

For a detailed account of the psychophysical methods developed by Fechner and others, see
  Woodworth, R. S., & Schlosberg, H. (1955). *Experimental psychology*. London: Methuen (chaps 8 and 9); or, even more comprehensive, Guilford, J. P. (1954). *Psychometric methods* (2nd edn). New York: McGraw-Hill.
For a definitive record of S. S. Stevens's contribution to psychophysics, see Stevens, S. S. (1975). *Psychophysics*. New York: Wiley.
For an account of recent developments in sensory discrimination, see Laming, D. (1986). *Sensory analysis*. London: Academic Press.

REFERENCES

Baird, J. C., Green, D. M., & Luce, R. D. (1980). Variability and sequential effects in cross-modality matching of area and loudness. *Journal of Experimental Psychology: Human Perception and Performance*, 6, 277–289.

Baird, J. C., Lewis, C., & Romer, D. (1970). Relative frequencies of numerical responses in ratio estimation. *Perception and Psychophysics*, *8*, 358–362.

Brown, W. (1910). The judgment of difference. *University of California Publications in Psychology*, *1*, 1–71.

Cornsweet, T. N. (1962). The staircase-method in psychophysics. *American Journal of Psychology*, *75*, 485–491.

Cornsweet, T. N. (1970). *Visual perception*. New York: Academic Press.

Fechner, G. T. (1860). *Elemente der Psychophysik* (2 vols). Leipzig: Breitkopf & Härtel. (Vol. 1 trans. by H. E. Adler (1966) *Elements of psychophysics*. New York: Holt, Rinehart & Winston.)

Jesteadt, W., Wier, C. C., & Green, D. M. (1977). Intensity discrimination as a function of frequency and sensation level. *Journal of the Acoustical Society of America*, *61*, 169–177.

Kellogg, W. N. (1929). An experimental comparison of psychophysical methods. *Archives of Psychology*, *17*, whole no. 106.

Kiesow, F. (1925/1926). Über die Vergleichung linearer Strecken und ihre Bezeihung zum Weberschen Gesetze. *Archiv für die gesamte Psychologie*, *52*, 61–90; *53*, 433–446; *56*, 421–451.

Krantz, D. H. (1971). Integration of just-noticeable differences. *Journal of Mathematical Psychology*, *8*, 591–599.

Laming, D. (1984). The relativity of 'absolute' judgements. *British Journal of Mathematical and Statistical Psychology*, *37*, 152–183.

Laming, D. (1986). *Sensory analysis*. London: Academic Press.

Laming, D. (1989). Experimental evidence for Fechner's and Stevens's laws. *Behavioral and Brain Sciences*, *12*, 277–281.

Laming, D. (1991). Reconciling Fechner and Stevens? *Behavioral and Brain Sciences*, *14*, 188–191.

Laming, D., & Marsh, D. (1988). Some performance tests of QUEST on measurements of vibrotactile thresholds. *Perception and Psychophysics*, *44*, 99–107.

Levitt, H. (1971). Transformed up-down methods in psychoacoustics. *Journal of the Acoustical Society of America*, *49*, 467–477.

Luce, R. D., & Edwards, W. (1958). The derivation of subjective scales from just noticeable differences. *Psychological Review*, *65*, 222–237.

Poulton, E. C. (1967). Population norms of top sensory magnitudes and S. S. Stevens' exponents. *Perception and Psychophysics*, *2*, 312–316.

Stephanowitsch, J. (1913). Untersuchung der Herstellung der subjektiven Gleichheit bei der Methode der mittleren Fehler unter Anwendung der Registriermethode. *Psychologische Studien*, *8*, 77–116.

Stevens, J. C., Mack, J. D., and Stevens, S. S. (1960). Growth of sensation on seven continua as measured by force of handgrip. *Journal of Experimental Psychology*, *59*, 60–67.

Stevens, S. S. (1936). A scale for the measurement of a psychological magnitude: Loudness. *Psychological Review*, *43*, 405–416.

Stevens, S. S. (1956). The direct estimation of sensory magnitudes – loudness. *American Journal of Psychology*, *69*, 1–25.

Stevens, S. S. (1957). On the psychophysical law. *Psychological Review*, *64*, 153–181.

Stevens, S. S. (1966). Matching functions between loudness and ten other continua. *Perception and Psychophysics*, *1*, 5–8.

Stevens, S. S. (1970). Neural events and the psychophysical law. *Science*, *170*, 1043–1050.

Stevens, S. S. (1971). Issues in psychophysical measurement. *Psychological Review*, *78*, 426–450.

Stevens, S. S. (1975). *Psychophysics*. New York: Wiley.

Stevens, S. S., & Greenbaum, H. B. (1966). Regression effect in psychophysical judgment. *Perception and Psychophysics, 1*, 439–446.

Swets, J. A., Tanner, W. P., & Birdsall, T. G. (1961). Decision processes in perception. *Psychological Review, 68*, 301–340.

Tanner, W. P., & Swets, J. A. (1954). A decision-making theory of visual detection. *Psychological Review, 61*, 401–409.

Teghtsoonian, R. (1971). On the exponents in Stevens' Law and the constant in Ekman's Law. *Psychological Review, 78*, 71–80.

Thurstone, L. L. (1927). A law of comparative judgment. *Psychological Review, 34*, 273–286.

Torgerson, W. S. (1958). *Theory and methods of scaling*. New York: Wiley.

Treisman, M. (1963). Temporal discrimination and the indifference interval: Implications for a model of the "internal clock". *Psychological Monographs, 77*(576).

Watson, A. B., & Pelli, D. G. (1983). QUEST: A Bayesian adaptive psychometric method. *Perception and Psychophysics, 33*, 113–120.

Weber, E. H. (1834). *De pulsu, resorptione, auditu et tactu. Annotctiones anatomicae et physiologicae*. Leipzig: Koehler. (Trans. H. E. Ross & D. J. Murray (1978) *The sense of touch*. London: Academic Press.)

Wier, C. C., Jesteadt, W., & Green, D. M. (1976). A comparison of method-of-adjustment and forced-choice procedures in frequency discrimination. *Perception and Psychophysics, 19*, 75–79.

GLOSSARY

This glossary is confined to a selection of frequently used terms that merit explanation or comment. Its informal definitions are intended as practical guides to meanings and usages. The entries are arranged alphabetically, word by word, and numerals are positioned as though they were spelled out.

absolute threshold in psychophysics (q.v.), the minimum physical energy of a sensory stimulus that allows it to be detected by an observer.

accommodation 1. in Piaget's theory of cognitive development, the type of adaptation in which old cognitive schemata are modified or new ones formed in order to absorb information that can neither be ignored nor adapted through assimilation into the existing network of knowledge, beliefs, and expectations. **2.** In vision, modification of the shape of the eye's lens to focus on objects at different distances. **3.** In social psychology, the modification of behaviour in response to social pressure or group norms, as for example in conformity.

ACTH *see* adrenocorticotropic hormone (ACTH).

action potential the momentary change in electrical potential that occurs when an impulse is propagated along a neuron (q.v.). Also called nerve impulse.

adaptation 1. in evolutionary theory, some feature of an organism's structure, physiology, or behaviour that solves a problem in its life. **2.** In sensory psychology, a temporary change in the responsiveness of a receptor as a result of an increase or decrease in stimulation. **3.** In social psychology, a general term for any process whereby people adapt their behaviour to fit in with a changed cultural environment.

adrenal glands from the Latin *ad*, to, *renes*, kidneys, a pair of endocrine glands (q.v.), situated just above the kidneys, which secrete adrenalin (epinephrine), noradrenalin (norepinephrine) (qq.v.), and other hormones into the bloodstream. See also adrenocorticotropic hormone (ACTH).

adrenalin(e) hormone secreted by the adrenal glands (q.v.), causing an increase in blood pressure, release of sugar by the liver, and several other physiological reactions to perceived threat or danger. *See also* endocrine glands, noradrenalin(e).

adrenocorticotropic hormone (ACTH) a hormone secreted by the pituitary gland that stimulates the adrenal gland to secrete corticosteroid hormones such as cortisol (hydrocortisone) into the bloodstream, especially in response to stress or injury.

afferent neurons from the Latin *ad*, to, *ferre*, to carry, neurons (q.v.) that transmit impulses from the sense organs to the central nervous system (CNS) (q.v.). *Cf.* efferent neurons.

anosmia loss of the sense of smell as a result of damage to the olfactory nerve or some other cause.

arousal a general term for an organism's state of physiological activation, mediated by the autonomic nervous system. *See also* Yerkes-Dodson law.

association areas parts of the cerebral cortex (q.v.) not primarily devoted to sensory or motor functions.

audition the sense of hearing.

auditory nerve the nerve connecting the auditory (hearing) receptors to the brain.

autokinetic movement from the Greek *autos*, self, *kinesis*, movement, a visual illusion involving the apparent movement of a stationary point of light viewed in a completely dark environment.

autonomic nervous system a subdivision of the nervous system that regulates (autonomously) the internal organs and glands. It is divided into the sympathetic nervous system and the parasympathetic nervous system (qq.v.).

axon from the Greek word meaning axis, a process or extending fibre of a neuron (q.v.) which conducts impulses away from the cell body and transmits them to other neurons.

basilar membrane the membrane in the inner ear in which the auditory receptor cells are embedded.

binocular disparity the slight difference between the two retinal images, due to the slightly different vantage points of the two eyes, which serves as the basis of stereoscopic depth perception.

bipolar cell a neuron (q.v.), usually a sensory nerve cell, with two processes, axon and dendrite (qq.v.), extending in opposite directions from the cell body.

bottom-up processing in cognitive psychology, information processing that "raw" sensory stimuli and then works up to more abstract cognitive operations, as for example in a computational theory (q.v.) of vision. *Cf.* top-down processing.

cell body sometimes called the *soma*, the central part of a neuron (q.v.), containing the nucleus and other structures that keep the cell alive.

central nervous system (CNS) in human beings and other vertebrates, the brain and spinal cord.

cerebellum from the Latin diminutive form of *cerebrum*, brain, one of the main divisions of the brain, situated beneath the back of the main part of the brain, involved in the regulation of movement and balance.

cerebral cortex from the Latin *cerebrum*, brain, *cortex*, bark, the thin layer of cells covering the cerebrum (q.v.), largely responsible for higher mental functions.

cerebrum from the Latin word meaning brain, the largest brain structure, comprising the front and upper part of the brain, of which the cortex (outer layer) controls most sensory, motor, and cognitive processes in human beings.

chemical senses the senses of olfaction (smell) and gustation (taste) (qq.v.).

cochlea from the Greek *kochlias*, snail, a fluid-filled spiral tube in the inner ear, shaped like the shell of a snail, containing the basilar membrane (q.v.) and the receptors for hearing that convert sound waves into nerve impulses.

cognition from the Latin *cognoscere*, to know, attention, thinking, problem-solving, remembering, and all other mental processes that fall under the general heading of information processing.

computational theory a formal approach to the study of vision, pioneered by David Marr in the late 1970s, which is intended to show how the pattern of light falling on the retinas of the eyes is transformed into a symbolic representation of the shapes, colours, and movements of what is observed. The first stage is the construction of the primal sketch based on individual intensity changes within a map based on the retina, with edge fragments grouped into meaningful clusters relating to surfaces; then depth cues are used to form the viewer-centred 2½D sketch, which is insufficient for object recognition because it is not invariant with respect to the observer's viewpoint; and the final stage is the construction of the object-centred 3D model description.

cone any of the conical cells in the retina of the eye, sensitive to bright light and colour. *Cf.* rod.

correlation in statistics, the relationship between two variables such that high scores on one tend to go with high scores on the other or (in the case of negative correlation) such that high scores on one tend to go with low scores on the other. The usual index of correlation, called the product-moment correlation coefficient and symbolized by *r*, ranges from 1.00 for perfect positive correlation, through zero for uncorrelated variables, to −1.00 for perfect negative correlation.

correlational study a non-experimental type of research design in which patterns of correlations (q.v.) are analysed.

dark adaptation the process by which the eyes adjust from bright light to low levels of illumination. The cones (q.v.) in the retina adapt within about seven minutes, and the rods (q.v.) within about four hours.

decibel (dB) a unit commonly used for measuring the physical intensity of sound, equal to ten times the logarithm to the base 10 of the ratio of the intensity of the sound to the intensity of a reference sound, usually the faintest sound audible under ideal listening conditions (conventionally 0.0002 dynes/cm^2).

dendrite from the Greek *dendron*, tree, the collection of branched, threadlike extensions of a neuron (q.v.) that receives impulses from other neurons or from a receptor and conducts them towards the cell body.

difference threshold in psychophysics (q.v.), the smallest difference in physical intensity between two stimuli (q.v.) that can be perceived.

echoic store the sensory memory (q.v.) register or store for auditory information. *Cf.* iconic store.

efferent neurons from the Latin *e*, from, *ferre*, to carry, neurons that transmit impulses away from the central nervous system (CNS) towards the muscles, glands, etc. *Cf.* afferent neurons.

eidetic image from the Greek *eidos*, shape, an exceptionally vivid, virtually "photographic" visual memory image, much more common among children than adults. The term is occasionally applied by analogy to auditory memories.

endocrine gland any ductless gland, such as the adrenal gland or pituitary gland (qq.v.), that secretes hormones (q.v.) directly into the bloodstream. The endocrine system functions as an elaborate signalling system within the body, alongside the nervous system (q.v.).

endorphins from the Greek *endon*, within, and morphine, from *Morpheus*, the Greek god of sleep and dreams, any of a class of morphine-like substances occurring naturally in the brain that bind to pain receptors and thus block pain sensations.

epinephrine, norepinephrine from the Greek *epi*, upon, *nephros*, kidney, alternative words for adrenalin and noradrenalin (qq.v.), especially in United States usage. *See also* endocrine gland.

feature detectors sensory neurons that are particularly responsive to specific features of stimuli, for example a line detector, a corner detector, or a voice-onset detector.

Fechner's law in psychophysics (q.v.), the law discovered by the German philosopher and mystic Gustav Theodor Fechner in 1850, which states that sensations increase by equal steps as stimulus intensity increases by equal proportions; this is usually expressed mathematically by stating that magnitude of sensation is a logarithmic

126

function of stimulus intensity: $\psi = k \log \phi$, where ψ is the magnitude of the sensation, ϕ is the physical intensity of the stimulus, and k is a constant. Cf. Weber's law.

ganglion cells neurons in the retina of the eye that receive impulses from receptor cells and whose axons constitute the optic nerve.

Gestalt psychology from the German *Gestalt*, configuration or form, a school of psychology that flourished in Germany from 1912 until the rise of the Nazis and emphasized the importance of studying patterns, configurations, and wholes, which are sometimes more than the sum of their parts, rather than isolated elements.

gustation from the Latin *gustare*, to taste, the sense of taste.

harmonics components of musical tones with frequencies that are integral multiples of the fundamental frequencies. The first harmonic of a tone is the fundamental itself, the second harmonic has twice the frequency of the fundamental and is sometimes called the first overtone, the third harmonic has three times the frequency of the fundamental and is the second overtone, and so on.

hormone from the Greek *horman*, to stir up or urge on, a chemical substance secreted into the bloodstream by an endocrine gland (q.v.) and transported to another part of the body where it exerts a specific effect.

iconic store from the Latin *icon*, image, the sensory memory register or store for visual information. *Cf.* echoic store. *See also* sensory memory.

just noticeable difference (jnd) in psychophysics (q.v.), the difference between two sensory stimuli that is only just detectable under ideal experimental conditions.

kinaesthesis from the Greek *kinein*, to move, *aisthesis*, feeling, the sensory modality, also called muscle sense, through which bodily position, weight, muscle tension, and movement are perceived.

long-term memory (LTM) relatively long-lasting memory for information that has been deeply processed. *Cf.* sensory memory, short-term memory (STM).

memory the mental processes of encoding, storage, and retrieval of information. *See also* long-term memory, sensory memory, short-term memory (STM).

muscle sense *see* kinaesthesis.

NA a common abbreviation for noradrenalin (q.v.).

NE a common abbreviation for norepinephrine. *See* noradrenalin.

nervous system *see under* autonomic nervous system, central nervous system (CNS), parasympathetic nervous system, sympathetic nervous system.

neuron from the Greek word for nerve, a nerve cell, which is the basic structural and functional unit of the nervous system, consisting of a cell body, axon, and dendrites (qq.v.). *See also* afferent neuron, efferent neuron.

neurophysiology the study of the operation of the nervous system (q.v.).

nocioceptor a receptor (q.v.), generally in the skin, sensitive to pain, sometimes called a nocioreceptor.

noradrenalin one of the catecholamine hormones and an important neurotransmitter in the nervous system, also called norepinephrine, especially in United States usage.

norepinephrine *see* noradrenalin.

olfaction the sense of smell.

opponent-process cells cells in the visual system that respond to light of a specific range of wavelengths and are actively inhibited from responding by other wavelengths.

optic chiasma the area in the brain behind the eyes where the optic nerves cross.

organ of Corti named after the nineteenth-century Italian anatomist Alfonso Corti, the array of tiny hair cells attached to the basilar membrane (q.v.) that form part of the auditory receptor in the inner ear and whose movements in response to sound waves trigger nerve impulses to the brain.

parasympathetic nervous system one of the two major divisions of the autonomic nervous system (q.v.); its general function is to conserve metabolic energy. *Cf.* sympathetic nervous system.

peptides chemical substances such as endorphins (q.v.) that regulate various bodily functions and play an important part in the experience of pain.

perception the processing of sensory information from the receptors (q.v.). *Cf.* sensation.

perceptual constancy the tendency for a perceived object, or a perceptual quality such as colour, to appear the same even when the pattern of sensory stimulation changes because of a change in orientation, distance, illumination, or some other influencing factor.

pinna the external part of the ear, sometimes called the auricle.

pituitary gland the master endocrine gland (q.v.), attached by a stalk to the base of the brain, which secretes into the bloodstream hormones affecting bodily growth and the functioning of other endocrine glands. *See also* adrenocorticotropic hormone (ACTH).

primal sketch *see under* computational theory.

product-moment correlation coefficient *see under* correlation.

psychology from the Greek *psyche*, mind, *logos*, study, the study of the nature, functions, and phenomena of behaviour and mental experience.

psychophysics the study of the functional relationships between physical properties of stimuli and psychological responses to them. *See also* absolute threshold, difference threshold, Fechner's law, just noticeable difference, signal detection theory, Weber's law.

receptor a sense organ or structure that is sensitive to a specific form of physical energy and that transmits neural information to other parts of the nervous system (q.v.).

response any behavioural or glandular activity of a person or an animal, especially as a reaction to a stimulus (q.v.).

retinal disparity *see* binocular disparity.

rod any of the elongated cylindrical cells in the retina of the eye, containing rhodopsin (visual purple) and sensitive to dim light but not to colour. *Cf.* cone.

semicircular canals the three looped, fluid-filled tubes, set at right angles to one another, that form the labyrinth of the inner ear and play a crucial role in the sense of orientation, balance, and movement.

sensation acquisition by the body's internal and external sense organs or receptors (q.v.) of "raw" information. *Cf.* perception.

sensory adaptation the diminution or disappearance of responsiveness that occurs when an unchanging stimulus (q.v.) is repeated or continued.

sensory deprivation an experimental situation in which sensory input to all receptors (q.v.) is severely reduced.

sensory memory a form of memory, necessary for normal vision and hearing, which allows visual images to be stored for about half a second and sounds for up to two seconds. Sensory memory enables television, which presents 30 still images per second, to convey the illusion of a single moving image. It also makes speech intelligible, because without it, by the end of each spoken word the hearer would have forgotten its beginning. *See also* sensory registers. Cf. long-term memory, short-term memory.

sensory registers subsystems of sensory memory (q.v.), such as (for vision) the iconic store and (for hearing) the echoic store (qq.v.), generally assumed to exist separately for each sensory modality.

short-term memory (STM) a memory store, also called working memory, consisting of a central executive, visuo-spatial sketchpad, and articulatory loop that is used for storing small amounts of information for periods of time ranging from a few seconds to a few minutes. It has a severely limited capacity of about seven or eight items of information, such as digits of a telephone number, and the information is rapidly forgotten unless it is refreshed by rehearsal, following which it may eventually be transferred to long-term memory (LTM) (q.v.). *See also* sensory memory.

signal detection theory a mathematical theory derived from psychophysics (q.v.) to explain the detection of a sensory signal, taking into account the intensity of the signal, the amount of background noise, the level of motivation of the subject, and the criterion for responding.

size-weight illusion a compelling illusion whereby, if two objects are of equal weight but markedly different sizes, the smaller object feels much heavier than the larger. Sometimes called Charpentier's illusion.

soma *see* cell body.

stereopsis the visual perception of objects in three dimensions, or stereoscopic vision.

stimulus (pl. stimuli) any objectively discernable event capable of evoking a response (q.v.) in an organism.

subjects from the Latin *sub*, under, *jacere*, to throw, people or other organisms whose behaviour or mental experience is investigated in psychological research.

subliminal from the Latin *sub*, beneath, *limen*, threshold, below the threshold of consciousness; used in perception for a stimulus of very small intensity or duration that can be shown to have been perceived without conscious awareness.

sympathetic nervous system one of the two major divisions of the autonomic nervous system; it is concerned with general activation, and it mobilizes the body's reaction to stress or perceived danger. *Cf.* parasympathetic nervous system.

thalamus from the Greek *thalamos*, an inner room or bedroom, a major interior brain structure that serves as a relay centre to the cerebral cortex for all sensory impulses except those arising from olfaction.

3D model description *see under* computational theory.

timbre from the Old French word meaning bell, the sound quality that distinguishes one spoken vowel from another, one voice from another, or one musical instrument from another when pitch and loudness are held constant.

top-down processing in cognitive psychology, information processing that proceeds from general assumptions or presuppositions about the material being processed. *Cf.* bottom-up processing.

trichromatic theory a theory of colour vision based on three primary colour receptors. *See also* Young-Helmholtz theory.

129

2½D sketch *see under* computational theory.

two-point threshold the minimum distance apart at which two pinpricks on a specified area of the body are perceived as two separate pricks.

Weber fraction *see under* Weber's law.

Weber's law in psychophysics (q.v.), the law of sensation discovered by the German physiologist Ernst Heinrich Weber in 1846, which states that the just noticeable difference between two stimuli is a constant fraction of the lesser stimulus; for example, the just noticeable difference between two weights is 1/53 of the lighter weight. Thus the Weber fraction for weight discrimination is 1/53; for visual brightness discrimination it is 1/62, for auditory pitch discrimination it is 1/333, for loudness discrimination it is 1/1 1, and so on. The usual mathematical expression of Weber's law is $\Delta I/I = k$, where ΔI is a small increment in the physical intensity of the stimulus, I is the initial stimulus intensity, and k is a constant equal to the Weber fraction. *Cf.* Fechner's law.

working memory *see* short-term memory (STM).

Yerkes-Dodson law a psychological law named after its proposers stating that optimal performance on a variety of tasks occurs at intermediate levels of arousal (q.v.).

Young-Helmholtz theory a theory of colour vision, named after its originators, which turned out to be essentially correct, based on the assumption that all colours are reducible to combinations of three basic colour components, each of which stimulates a specific receptor (q.v.) in the retina of the eye.

INDEX